WEALTH
FOR THE
REST OF US

by Terry Bontemps

Subscribe to Terry Bontemps' YouTube Channel
https://www.youtube.com/user/ibuyhouses1

Limits of Liability and Disclaimer of Warranty:

The author and publisher shall not be liable for your misuse of this material. This book is strictly for informational and educational purposes.

Warning – Disclaimer:

The purpose of this book is to educate and entertain. The author and/ or publisher do not guarantee that anyone following these techniques, suggestions, tips, ideas, or strategies will become successful. The author and/or publisher shall have neither liability nor responsibility to anyone with respect to any loss or damage caused, or alleged to be caused, directly or indirectly by the information contained in this book.

Bank Foreclosure Millionaire™

TAKE ACTION AND IMPLEMENT THE INFORMATION IN MY BOOK LIKE IT'S GOING TO MAKE YOU MORE SUCCESSFUL FINANCIALLY THAN YOU'VE EVER, EVER, EVER BEEN BEFORE IN YOUR LIFE!

Follow the 15 steps below to learn Terry Bontemps' real estate and wealth-building methodology:

1. Read Terry Bontemps' book, "Wealth For The Rest of Us" to learn his real estate methodology

2. Watch Terry Bontemps' videos to understand his proprietary strategies.

3. Download Terry Bontemps' mobile app, Bank Foreclosure Millionaire, from the Amazon or Apple Store.

4. Use the app to access the author's wealth-building real estate education game, which teaches the intricate details of making money through real estate investing.

5. Tap the "Click Here First" button to receive mentorship from Terry Bontemps at each level of his real estate education game.

6. Watch Terry Bontemps demonstrate his app to learn how to make money.

7. Practice and implement the investment strategies taught by Terry Bontemps using his app.

8. Start at Level 1 as a real estate investor (wholesaler) and learn how to find great deals and flip them to investors for a fee.

9. Progress to Level 2 as a fix and flipper and learn how to rehab houses and sell them for a profit.

10. Advance to Level 3 as a landlord and learn how to generate passive income through rental properties.

11. Pay $19.99 to access Levels 4 through 8, where you will learn about note-buying, borrowing money from money partners, flipping notes and REOs to hedge funds, Airbnb & residential assisted living.

12. Utilize the app's resources, such as videos and articles, to further enhance your knowledge and understanding of real estate investing.

13. Stay committed and consistent in your learning and implementation of the Terry's strategies to achieve financial freedom and build generational wealth.

14. Educate your children about money, finances, and real estate investment using Terry Bontemps' app.

15. If you want personal mentorship from Terry Bontemps, call him at (916) 470-3869.

CAUTION: THE CONTENT IN THIS BOOK CONTAINS LIFE-CHANGING INFORMATION!
Real estate is the vehicle that can make you as wealthy as you want to be. Just duplicate for yourself the investment strategies I'm teaching you in my book and take ACTION!

DISRUPT
THE TRADITIONAL CRITERIA FOR BUILDING WEALTH

TO DISRUPT MEANS TO CHALLENGE THE NORM. TO CHALLENGE WHAT PEOPLE NORMALLY THINK ABOUT WEALTH, WHAT THEY SAY ABOUT WEALTH AND WHAT THEY NORMALLY DO ABOUT ACQUIRING WEALTH The statis quo is the current state of things. If you are already wealthy, then you're most likely not interested in disrupting the status quo...

WEALTH HAS BEEN AN EXCLUSIONARY PROPOSITION

For far too long, those who don't have wealth, have been excluded from having any damn thing!

So, wealth in and of itself is typically the province of those who already have wealth.

WHAT ABOUT WEALTH FOR THE REST OF US?

Terry Bontemps

A movement is a concept or idea that people rally around… Every movement must be disruptive and it's the disruptive moments in your movement that give it momentum. To disrupt means to challenge the norm. To challenge what people normally think about wealth, what they say about wealth, and what they normally do about wealth!

- Trevor Otts

THE GOAL OF EVERY WOMAN SHOULD BE FINANCIAL FREEDOM

You've always wanted to try your hand at real estate, you've always wanted to provide for your family and honesty you are just tired of living on the edge financially.

It's time for change

It's time for action not self doubt

It's time for follow thru as opposed to another missed opportunity

BETHATWEALTHYWOMAN.COM

FREE 30 MINUTE DISCOVERY CALL
TEXT MENTOR
(916)470-3869

TABLE OF CONTENTS

Meet
TERRY BONTEMPS

With over 40 years of experience as a Real Estate professional, Terry has seen firsthand how real estate investing can deliver unbelievable financial gains in as little as a few weeks, and has decided to share his trade-secrets, industry tips, and tricks with the public!

Maybe you're thinking, "Sure it worked for Terry, but who's to say it'll work for me?"

I'm glad you asked!

Past students have earned:

- $1.2 Million in only 1 hour!
- $400,000 in only 9 months!
- $1.5 Million in only 10 months!
- $2,100 residual monthly income!

Click the link below or scan the QR code to hear from past successful students

https://www.buyingforeclosuresfrombanks.com/video-testimonial-page

DISRUPT

THE TRADITIONAL CRITERIA FOR BUILDING WEALTH

TO DISRUPT MEANS TO CHALLENGE THE NORM. TO CHALLENGE WHAT
PEOPLE NORMALLY THINK ABOUT WEALTH, WHAT THEY SAY ABOUT
WEALTH AND WHAT THEY NORMALLY DO ABOUT ACQUIRING WEALTH
The statis quo is the current state of things. If you are already wealthy,
then you're most likely not interested in disrupting the status quo...

The historical truth about how the middle class, the poor, minorities and marginalized communities have been systematically shut out of building wealth, and what you need to do about it

We have a wealth inequality problem in this country that's not easily solvable. One of the biggest problems associated with wealth in the United States is the lack of inclusion of the middle class and the poor. Wealth is not finding its way into the pockets of the average American. When you look at many of the wealth-building strategies out there, the reality is oftentimes that they automatically exclude most of us, and we feel that exclusion every day.

Wealth is typically the province of the people who already have it, and it rarely gives the people who don't have wealth the opportunity to have any damn thing. At the end of the day, wealth excludes the have-nots.

When you don't have wealth, you don't get a chance for better schooling for your family. When you don't have wealth, you don't get a chance for better housing and health care. The current financial system excludes the majority of Americans because wealth in and of itself is exclusionary.

WEALTH FOR THE REST OF US is for the rest of us who are not wealthy. There's the wealthy, the middle class and the poor; most of us fall into the bottom two… specifically, there's not enough wealth for the rest of us. My book is aimed primarily at minorities, marginalized communities, the middle class and the poor because wealth typically excludes this segment of society.

1

WEALTH FOR THE REST OF US is for you if you want wealth and you feel like you've been EXCLUDED from the wealth-building process. Most of the wealth-building strategies on the market are predicated on your need to have money in the bank and good credit.

WEALTH FOR THE REST OF US is for the 78% of the people in the United States who are living paycheck-to-paycheck.

WEALTH FOR THE REST OF US is for the people who have dreams and aspirations and are trying to include themselves in the wealth creation conversation. A conversation about a better life, better schooling, better health care, better opportunities for their families, and the chance to live the American dream.

WEALTH FOR THE REST OF US is for the 57% of Black families, 28% of White families, 50% of Hispanic families, 39% of Asian families, and other nationalities who are being locked out of the opportunity to own a home, invest in real estate, own property, build generational wealth, and live the American dream due to not being able to access capital, credit, and financial opportunities.

According to *The Washington Post*, one in seven White families are millionaires, while only one out of 50 Black families are millionaires. What about wealth for the rest of us who are not millionaires?

WEALTH FOR THE REST OF US is for those of us who don't understand and were not taught that the traditional wealth-building investment strategies and conventional financial advice that's on the market was developed mainly for the wealthy by people who are already wealthy. Those investment strategies don't work for the REST OF US.

WEALTH FOR THE REST OF US is for you if someday you want to get to the point at which you don't have to work for money anymore.

WEALTH FOR THE REST OF US is for the rest of us who are not accredited investors. It's for the rest of us who don't have an annual income of $200,000 ($300,000 couples), or a net worth of $1 million or more.

Accredited investor requirements rule out most of the U.S. population from investing because the median income is far too low, at approximately $67,500 in 2020, according to government data.

So, how do you generate wealth coming from the position you are in life? Is there a financial plan that takes everyday people that are un-bankable to wealth from where their current financial status is in life?

WHAT IF there was a wealth-building platform that INCLUDES instead of excludes the poor, the middle class, and the 78% of people living paycheck-to-paycheck with zero barriers. That's not predicated on what you have in your bank account, your credit score, your education level, your previous investing experience, and without getting loans from banks?

Over the last 40 years of investing and 21 years of teaching others how to build wealth in real estate, I've developed a wealth-building platform that makes it highly possible for people with an average income to generate real wealth with what they're working with.

From investing in six different real estate markets, including California, Nevada, Arizona, Illinois, Florida, and New York, I've developed a plan that is not predicated on you having a million dollars in the bank, $100,000, $500, or even $5 in the bank. It's not predicated on your credit score, previous experience, dealing with realtors, or qualifying for loans and borrowing money from banks.

My game plan is predicated on understanding how to use other people's money and using real estate strategies in a way that allows people to generate real wealth for themselves and their families, just like my student Ron, who made $1.2 million in one hour, and Holly, who made $400,000 in nine months and increased her net worth $1.5 million dollars in 10 months using my real estate platform.

So many deserving people are being locked out of the wealth-building experience due to what they don't know and/or because of their current financial situation. The reason most of us exclude ourselves from the conversation about having wealth, investing in real estate, and owning a home is because of how much money we have or don't have in our bank account, and our credit score. For most people, wealth has eluded them because they were missing the savvy, the right strategy, the mentorship, the consistency, and the know-how.

3

My name is Terry Bontemps, and I didn't know what I didn't know when it came to generating wealth. Like many others before me, I thought I needed money and credit, influence and relationships when all I needed was the know-how. So, I started learning everything I could about bank foreclosure notes. I went from the student, to the teacher, to the expert, to the world's #1 bank foreclosure mentor. I was able to rescue my family from a life of financial hardship. I was able to finally start living the lifestyle I used to only dream about. I was able to create true financial freedom and happiness all because I was willing, ready, and committed to the wealth-building process.

We all should be wealthy… that is why I created this amazing book, titled *Wealth For The Rest Of Us*. It's the battle cry of the middle class and the poor. *Wealth For The Rest Of Us* is my movement, whose mission is to make wealth accessible, equitable, and inclusive for everyone, not just the wealthy with zero barriers regardless of your credit score, how much you have in your bank account, and your previous investing experience.

Here's what we know about wealth in the United States. The fastest path to wealth in the United States or any other country for that matter, that's been proven over and over again, has been owning real estate.

My reason for writing this book is to help people with financial literacy so they can improve their family's wealth and financial stability. So, don't worry about the money. Don't worry about your credit. I'm going to teach you everything you need to know about how to get started investing, making money, and building wealth owning real estate. I'm an advocate for the wealth champion in you. Together, we can make wealth accessible, equitable, and inclusive for everyone, not just the wealthy.

Wishing You Success, Health, Wealth, Happiness, and Prosperity!

Terry Bontemps

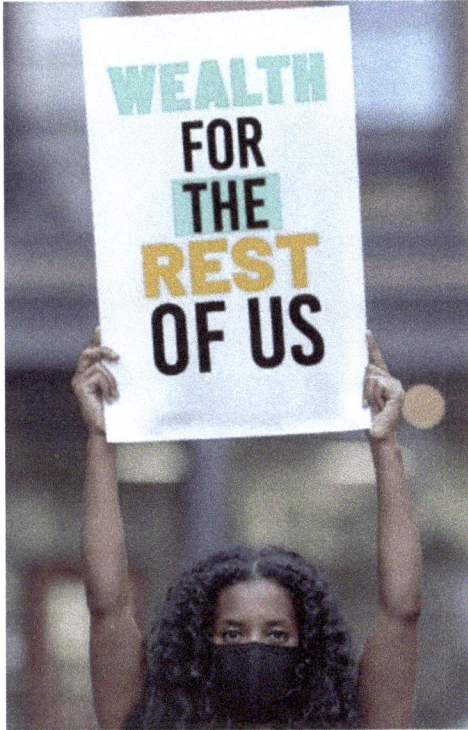

Click the video link below or scan the QR code to watch video
https://www.youtube.com/watch?v=Q7I1eWWNbJs

Wealth For The Rest Of Us is the compelling reason people buy into the brand, care about the brand and want to be a part of the movement.

Wealth For The Rest Of Us is not a little strategy or new get-rich gimmick that can show you how to make money.

Wealth For The Rest Of Us is a whole movement for anyone wanting wealth.

FOREWORD

Too many people have been locked out of the wealth game—until now.

Wealth for the Rest of Us **is a practical, step-by-step guide to achieving financial security, achieving the debt-free dream, and creating true generational wealth through real estate investing.**

For centuries, wealth in America has been reserved for and accessible by a chosen few. But for the rest of us? Wealth remains an unattainable goal and a game that many have never been allowed to play.

There are people who were born wealthy… and then there's the rest of us. There are people who have a certain background and live in a particular neighborhood… and then there's the rest of us. There are people who have the right education, credit score, and bank balance… and then there's the rest of us. Today, times have changed, and the tables have turned. Welcome to the redistribution of wealth.

Wealth for the Rest of Us levels the playing field and shows you how to make and multiply money, regardless of what you have – or don't.

In this book, Terry Bontemps – bank note buying real estate expert, wealth mentor, and self- made millionaire – shares the strategies he's used to build his own real estate empire and to coach his students through their own journeys to multiple-million-dollar real estate portfolios.

Inside, you'll learn:

- The historical truth about how minorities, the middle class and poor have been systematically shut out of building wealth – and what we need to do about it.

- The reason why you will work for the rest of your life and never be financially free unless you start thinking and doing differently right now.

- The money-making strategies that the banks and the financial powers that be never wanted you to know.

- Why the "fix and flip" approach to real estate investing will only drain your bank account instead of building it.
- The secret language of banks and how to learn in so you can start making (and multiplying) real money through real estate.

While most real estate millionaires remain silent about how they really made their money, Terry teaches you exactly how big deals are done. It's time to achieve true financial freedom (in your lifetime) and change the trajectory of your family finances forever.

—Stephanie Manns

The #1 way to acquire wealth in the world, not just the United States, is through property acquisition

But most of us exclude ourselves from the conversation around wealth due to how much money we have in our bank account

Or due to the fact we don't feel we have the proper credentials

Learn how to make money, build wealth, and be a real estate millionaire. Teach your kids and teens about money, finance, and investing. Download Terry's mobile app Bank Foreclosure Millionaire from Amazon or Apple Store today, $19.99.

ENDORSEMENTS

I believe that everyone does deserve to be financially free, and this topic of generational wealth is something worth talking about.

—Dr. Yang, California

Wealth For The Rest Of Us… is such a powerful concept and a deeper meaning than what the average person could really wrap their head around. After working with Terry and learning from him, I cannot wait to dive into his book.

When I first joined Terry's coaching program, I was with other real estate investing programs that taught you how to make money fixing and flipping property. I showed Terry a spreadsheet deal calculator that I received from one of the real estate education companies. I thought it was so sophisticated.

Terry wasn't impressed! He told me that he would have me create my own calculator. I didn't believe him. After about six coaching sessions with Terry, I had created my own deal analyzer calculator. I actually understood what each line item represented. I understood how each key performance indicator correlated with the others.

After about ten coaching sessions, I was able to completely reverse engineer this deal analyzer calculator that Terry helped me develop. I was also able to compute various profits for different types of real estate investment deals with one input of numbers.

As I advanced through his mentoring program, I understood every key performance indicator and was able to fully incorporate the information into my own deal calculator. I was able to easily evaluate a real estate deal in my head. One of the most important things I have learned from Terry is the concept of owing the note and "Being The Bank."

"Being The Bank" resonated with me and made me fully understand the difference between owning the note versus owning the property. Terry taught me that the owner of the note, which is the bank, doesn't have to make or pay for any repairs on the property. The owner of the note, which is the bank, does not have to take out the trash, replace the roof, mow the lawn, or call the plumber. This statement puts things in full perspective.

Had I not met Terry, I would be a two-trick pony. I would only be able to do what all of the other gurus preach and teach, which is wholesaling, and fix and flip real estate. These same real estate gurus teach you about generational wealth, but I have seen first-hand what wholesaling and fix and flipping has done to me, other investors and friends of mine.

Let me tell you, their way of teaching you how to invest in real estate definitely does not create generational wealth. All this did for me was create headaches and predatory hard money lenders chasing you down for interest only payments... in addition to imposing crazy penalties and expensive fees when you need an extension. Owning the note and being the bank is the best financial advice that I've ever heard. and Terry drives it home in his coaching program. Terry has dispelled the traditional myth and conventional wisdom that the only way to becoming wealthy is to have excellent credit, qualify for loans from banks, and have a bunch of money in your account.

Most of the wealth-building programs on the market require capital, credit, and previous investing experience. No one will tell you this. Everyone will just tell you about the shiny objects that they're using to sell their programs. *Wealth For The Rest of Us* is about you becoming your own bank instead of you and your family being enslaved financially to the banks. I cannot wait to get my hands on the book.

—Maurice C, Pennsylvania Real Estate Agent

Wealth For The Rest Of Us is long overdue. After knowing and watching your wealth-building application of investment strategies and wealth-acquisition techniques, I am excited all this knowledge can be shared with the rest of us.

My own personal wealth journey took a much longer time than I expected. I relied on old school applications of earning it, saving it, using the 10% rule, and perseverance. However, that rule is not always sustainable when you have a family whose needs change on a regular basis, and it definitely leaves little room for generational wealth.

Fortunately, through education and vision I realized such wealth cannot be earned working for someone else everyday but primarily through asset appreciation, primarily while you sleep. However, you must first obtain the assets and that is where leveraging comes into play.

If early in my career I had the benefit of such precise methodologies, I would have been further along much sooner in my wealth quest journey. I am excited that Terry's book *Wealth For The Rest Of Us* is finally here. With my guidance, it will serve as a beacon for my children and grandchildren toward making certain they maximize their wealth potential.

My goal is to see them reach for the moon and if they land on a star, then their wealth will still be riding high.

—Leon H, California Accountant

Hi Terry!

I've listened to your introductory audio for your upcoming book, ***Wealth For The Rest Of Us***. I'm intrigued and want to learn more myself! Thanks for sharing, and I look forward to reading the book and learning from you as well!

So far, it's definitely catchy, and I believe that everyone does deserve to be financially free, and this topic of generational wealth is something worth talking about and discussing how to break the barriers.

Looking forward to the rest of the book!

—Dr. Yang, California

Why is Wealth Often Exclusionary and Difficult to Attain?

Wealth is often exclusionary and difficult to attain for several reasons:

1. **Traditional Wealth Building Strategies**: Many traditional wealth building strategies were developed by the wealthy for people who already have wealth. These strategies often require having money in the bank, great credit and previous investing experience, which excludes those who don't have access to these resources.

2. **Lack of Access to Capital:** A significant barrier to wealth accumulation is the inability to access capital. Without money or credit, it becomes challenging to build wealth as many opportunities require financial resources.

3. **Limited Income and Financial Struggles**: A large portion of the population barely makes enough money to survive and pay bills, making it difficult to save, invest, and buy a home. Living paycheck to paycheck makes it difficult to accumulate wealth.

4. **Wealth Inequality**: There is a wealth inequality problem in many countries, including the United States. Wealth tends to concentrate in the hands of the already wealthy, leaving little opportunity for the middle class and the poor to accumulate wealth.

5. **Exclusion from Financial Opportunities**: Not having wealth excludes individuals and families from pursuing financial opportunities, such as better schooling, housing, and healthcare. This exclusion perpetuates a cycle of limited opportunities for those without wealth.

6. **Limited Access to Homeownership and Real Estate Investment**: A significant percentage of Americans, such as 57% of Black Americans, 28% of White Americans, 50% of Hispanic Americans, and 39% of Asian Americans, are being locked out of the opportunity to own a home, invest in real

estate, and build generational wealth. This lack of access to assets hinders wealth accumulation.

7. **Lack of Financial Literacy and Education**: Financial literacy and education are crucial for building wealth and making informed financial decisions. The majority of people have limited access to financial education resources and they may not have been exposed to financial concepts and investment strategies. This lack of knowledge can hinder their ability to make sound financial decisions and build wealth.

8. **Dependence On A Job**: Relying solely on a job for income is unlikely to make someone wealthy. Working for money alone does not lead to financial freedom. Wealth is generated by multiplying money through investments and other wealth-building strategies.

9. **Limited Opportunities for Inheritance**: The expectation of receiving a significant inheritance from a wealthy relative is often unrealistic. Inheriting wealth is not a reliable or accessible path to wealth for most individuals.

Overall, wealth is exclusionary and difficult to attain due to systemic barriers, limited access to resources, income disparities, and a lack of knowledge and opportunities.

There's a deeper spiritual understanding as to why you need to acquire wealth in your life

It's about you embracing the bigger picture around wealth

Why you want wealth, who you want wealth for and what you can do with it

Learn how to make money, build wealth, and be a real estate millionaire. Teach your kids and teens about money, finance, and investing. Download Terry's mobile app Bank Foreclosure Millionaire from Amazon or Apple Store today, $19.99.

DISRUPT
THE TRADITIONAL CRITERIA FOR BUILDING WEALTH

TO DISRUPT MEANS TO CHALLENGE THE BANKING AND REAL ESTATE INDUSTRY'S OPPRESIVE ECONOMIC SYSTEM THAT'S MEANT TO MINIMIZE AND MARGINALIZE THE MIDDLE CLASS & THE POOR: BANKS AND THE REAL ESTATE INDUSTRY PERPETUATE THE MYTH THAT PEOPLE WHO DON'T HAVE CREDIT, CAPITAL, & EXPERIENCE CAN'T OWN A HOME, INVEST IN REAL ESTATE & BUILD GENERATIONAL WEALTH

The statis quo is the current state of things. If you are already wealthy, then you're most likely not interested in disrupting the status quo...

WE ALL SHOULD BE WEALTHY!

IF YOU ONLY READ ONE CHAPTER OF MY BOOK, THIS IS THE ONE YOU WANT TO READ

My daughter was ready for college. She wanted to go to Arizona State University, and I couldn't pay for it! That was my motivation to succeed. It was time to Get Rich or Die Tryin.

—Terry Bontemps

Everybody knows what a two-by-four is, right? This two-by-four is symbolic of when my daughter wanted to go to college, and I didn't have the money. When she said, "Daddy, I'm ready for college, and I need money," bam, it felt like somebody had hit me in the head with a two-by-four.

There's the conventional way to invest in real estate, and the unconventional way. What I mean by conventional is you can go to the bank, you can get a loan, you can work with a realtor, and you can get a prequalification letter. You can get loans and borrow money from banks. You have great credit, a job, and money in the bank, which is the traditional criteria for building wealth.

Then, there's the unconventional way of investing in real estate. You may not have great credit, money in the bank, or a job, or you can't qualify to get loans and borrow money from banks. You can still own a home, invest, and build wealth in real estate, but you have to know the right strategies to use. Very few people know how to work with unconventional investors like I do.

YOU DON'T NEED MONEY, CREDIT, A JOB, OR TO BORROW MONEY AND GET LOANS FROM BANKS TO MAKE MONEY AND BUILD WEALTH INVESTING IN REAL ESTATE

The strategies I use to invest in real estate work for both, whether you're conventional or unconventional. I want the people that have financial challenges, that have issues, I call it being in the struggle. I want you to know that it was me, okay? I didn't have it made on a silver platter. I didn't have it. I had two foreclosures on my credit report, and from

18

the strategies I teach, I was able to buy and own real estate all over the United States. I came from nothing to be who I am today.

So, if you've got credit issues, you have money problems, you can't get loans and borrow money from banks, you can still be wealthy. You can still pass on generational wealth to your family. Here's the thing… you can't do it conventional-wise. You can't go to realtors and ask them to help you buy property because you're not qualified conventionally.

You can't go to the bank to get a loan because you're not qualified, but there is another way. They are going to tell you to clean up your credit, and save your money, then come back and see them.

If you want to buy real estate and build wealth today, you have to learn and do what I do in the unconventional world. Now, I'm not talking badly against realtors. I like realtors. I use realtors to sell my houses, but realtors can't help you if you're not conventional.

$1 MILLION DOLLARS OF GENERATIONAL WEALTH FOR ME FROM ONE STRATEGY MY MENTOR TAUGHT ME

If you're unconventional, realtors cannot help you, but there is a way, and I'm going to show you a $1 million property that I was able to pick up. I did not use a bank. I did not use a realtor. I didn't use my own money. That was in 1999, and today that property is worth $600,000. So, if I had listened to a realtor or listened to a banker, I wouldn't have been able to buy that property and build generational wealth for my family and me. Again, full disclosure: not talking badly against realtors, but they just don't have a program for you that are unconventional. So, I want to make sure if you're unconventional, you're struggling right now, and you need to make some money, let me tell you, real estate is the way to go, and I'm the guy to be your mentor to show you how.

I want to tell you how important it is to have a mentor. I had three mentors who were very influential in my life. There was my friend Carl Dexter, Ron LeGrand, and my uncle Austin. I'm going to tell you all a story about each one of my mentors.

First of all, let me just be straight up front and honest with you: there are only two ways you are going to learn how to invest in real estate. It's either going to be through the school of hard knocks by doing-it-by yourself, or you can get a mentor. You make up your mind. I'm just here to let you know what has made me successful, and why I'm the guy I am today, and it's because of the mentors that I've had in my life. I love them, the gurus!

I love them because they showed me a vision. I was just a normal guy working at a dead-end job who wanted more out of life, and real estate was the vehicle to that better life.

The mentors showed me a vision of what is possible, and I'm glad I went to the seminars. I'm glad I whipped out the credit cards because, guess what? Real estate works. You know it, and I know it; we just have to get it to work for you. There are plenty of people doing really well investing in real estate. Just look at HGTV. Just look at YouTube. Look at all the people making money in real estate. I've got over 400 videos on YouTube myself.

So, if you want to do some research on me, just go to YouTube. Punch in my name. So, I'm going to tell you about my daughter Tiffany. Everybody has someone in their family or a friend, like my daughter Tiffany. Tiffany was ready for college, but I didn't have the money because I was broke.

LET REAL ESTATE PAY FOR EVERYTHING YOU WANT IN LIFE!

She told me, "Daddy, I want to go to college," and I knew I didn't have the money to pay for it. I said, "The heck with that. I'm going back to real estate, and I'm going to get really serious about being wealthy."

Someone may be depending on you to provide the finances to help them achieve their dreams and goals. Real estate can pay for your family members' dreams. I love real estate because it's paid for me and my family's highest dreams and aspirations. That's what's so exciting. I've got 40 years of real estate experience, and I'm super pumped, super excited about real estate, because it changed my life!

You can do it yourself, or you can get a mentor. You're going to pay the price one way or the other. One time doing it yourself, and you make a mistake, you could've paid for a mentor.

LEAVING AN INHERITANCE AND PASSING WEALTH DOWN TO YOUR FAMILY MEMBERS

Let's talk about leaving a legacy for your family. We have an estate plan set up in an revocable living trust, so if and when something happens to me, my assets go to my family. I have it in a trust because I don't want my family's affairs to be public information that anybody can see.

If you're reading this and you own real estate, please, please, please, please, please put your properties in a revocable trust for asset protection because if you get into a lawsuit, that lawsuit is going to attach to all the properties that you own. Your real estate empire could be taken away from you by lawyers and that lawsuit.

I bought my first house when I was 20 years old in 1980. I've been around a long time, you guys. I teach men and women just like you how to invest in real estate, make money, build wealth, and be millionaires.

Yep, that's right. I say that because my students are making some of the most money per deal in the United States. My students have made over $4 million in profits. My top student made $1.2 million in one hour.

He bought a foreclosure property from the bank. It was a commercial foreclosure property – $1.2 million in one hour! Another one of my students made $400,000 in nine months buying these foreclosure properties directly from banks. She increased her net worth by $1.5 million, and she has $2,100 a month of rental income. They did it because I taught them how to invest in real estate, buying notes from banks.

BUYING FORECLOSURE PROPERTIES DIRECTLY FROM BANKS 40% TO 50% BELOW MARKET VALUE WITH NO MONEY OR CREDIT

This is what I'm an expert at. I'm a leading authority on buying foreclosure properties from banks. I'm the number one bank foreclosure mentor in the United States. I've been doing this since 2001. I've bought from banks in Arizona, Nevada, California, New York, Florida, and Illinois.

One time I tried to buy 174 loans from a bank in Oakland, California, that was valued at $40 million, which is the largest deal so far that I've ever worked on.

I was going to flip those loans to a hedge fund. If you're a wholesaler, check this out. Buying 174 loans from a bank and flipping them or wholesaling them to a hedge fund.

The hedge fund offered $22 million. I would've got a 1% flip fee, which is $220,000. That deal didn't go through but, boy, did I learn a lot about banks and hedge funds!

I've learned to make profits in real estate by being the bank. I buy these loans, and then I become the new bank of the homeowner. I do this to help homeowners facing foreclosure "keep their homes" instead of losing their homes at the auction.

So, let's say someone's in foreclosure and they're making their payments to Wells Fargo. I'd buy their loan from Wells Fargo, and then that person now has to make their payments to me, the bank of Terry Bontemps, not Wells Fargo.

I'M DEBT FREE... I DON'T OWE BANKS ANY MONEY, I'M THE BANK!

I don't owe banks any money on my properties, because I am the bank. I own my rental properties free and clear. I have no debt on my rental properties. I own my home free and clear. I have no debt. Why? Because I want those interest payments that the banks are making their money on.

I want that money that the banks are getting for me and my family. Terry Bontemps is a bank. I don't have any automobile debt. I don't have any student loan debt. I don't have any credit card debt. I am debt-free! There's no true freedom like financial freedom!

I'm going to tell you why I became debt-free. It's in my story. Again, I told you guys I built generational wealth for my family. I've achieved financial freedom. There's no true freedom like financial freedom.

I started with nothing, scratch, zero, but I saw an infomercial on TV. You've seen those real estate infomercials on TV, right? Come to this real estate seminar, yes, and we will show you how to do real estate.

So, I go because I'm broke and ready to quit my dead-end job – plus they were giving away some freebies from attending. If nothing else, I was hoping the freebies would teach me how to be wealthy. They said, "Hey, Terry, sit right up here in the front row."

I said, "Yes, I will, because I want to get what you guys are talking about. I want some of that stuff that real estate is able to afford." The seminar starts, and then they say, "Okay, Terry, now we're going to have another seminar this weekend in three days, and you got to pay X number of dollars."

I said, "Okay, let's do this." I whipped out that credit card, you guys. I sure did!

You know what I told him? "Look, try it on this credit card. You might have to put some on another credit card to cover the balance, and if I need more, well, I'm going to have to figure it out."

I was working at a dead-end job for a boss who was working me to death around the clock, and I was still broke working at that job. No matter how many hours I worked, the money was never enough for me to get ahead in life.

I PAID $1,200 FOR MY FIRST NOTE DEAL THAT I BOUGHT FROM A BANK AND I MADE $9,227 ONE YEAR LATER AND I DIDN'T KNOW WHAT I WAS DOING!

In that one seminar, the guy said, buy notes, buy foreclosures, buy the paper from banks and you could end up owning the real estate. From buying the note from the bank, you could end up owning the home which bypasses the conventional way most people buy real estate. I had no clue what he was talking about. See, that's a benefit of having a mentor. I didn't know that. I wasn't smart enough. I didn't graduate from college. I didn't understand that. He said, "Go buy the note!"

So, what did I do? I went back and started trying to buy these things called notes. The guy I'm talking about had bought over 2,000 houses, you guys. So, who am I not to listen to this smart person, especially when I paid all that money to learn how to invest in real estate? That's what I do. I find smart people; I get around them, and for information so they can make my world better.

What I learned in that seminar worked! I bought my first foreclosure property from a bank. I paid $1,200 for a note, and it was a third mortgage.

If you know anything about notes, a third mortgage is in a dangerous position, but I didn't know any better. I just did what the instructor at the seminar told me to do.

So, I bought that note. I sat on it for a year. I didn't know what to do. I can't remember what the teacher told me to do once I bought it.

One year later, I get a phone call. It's the title company. The title company says, "Hey, the homeowners are selling their house. They owe you some money for the note you own."

I go, "Well, how do you figure it out? I don't even know how to do this stuff." They said, "Bring your paperwork in. The reason we know you're the lien holder is because you have a lien recorded against the property as the bank."

Found out I was owed $9,227. I didn't touch the property. I didn't fix and flip it. I didn't go to Lowe's. I didn't go to Home Depot. I didn't have to deal with contractors. I didn't deal with tenants, toilets, or trash. I didn't have to pay any closing costs. I didn't have to manage the property, sell it, or pay any real estate agents commissions. Bigger than all this is I didn't need any credit, or I didn't need to qualify for any loans.

Boom. I made $9,227 in profits because I was the bank. Now, that probably doesn't sound like a lot of money to you, but I'm going to talk to you about return on investment, which we, as real estate investors, should understand thoroughly.

That was a 768% return on my money. That $1,200 investment made me $9,227 in one year for a 768% ROI on my money. For every dollar I invested in buying that note, I made $7.68. I multiplied my investment seven times.

HOW MUCH IS YOUR INVESTMENT $1,200	MULTIPLIED INVESTMENT 7.6X
HOW MUCH IS YOUR PROFIT $9,227	TIME TO GET BACK INVESTMENT 1 year
PROFIT MARGIN % N/A	BUYING REAL ESTATE ON THE $1 .13 cents on the dollar
WHAT'S YOUR ROI 768%	EQUITY N/A
EVERY $1 INVESTED WILL MAKE $7.68	PAYBACK PERIOD (cash flow) N/A

Money's Not Everything,
It's Just All We Talk About!

The rich don't work for money. We all know that. They don't have jobs. They have money work for them.

Real estate is something I've been teaching for the last 19 years. This is not a TED talk. This is not some Toastmasters speech. Real estate investing is something I've been doing for the last 43 years.

In order for you to build wealth and have wealth, you have to know how wealth is built, and 90% of this country's millionaires created their wealth in real estate.

When I heard that, I was like, "Dang, I can get in that group. You know what I mean?" 100% it's automatic for me, but 90%, I think I'm pretty intelligent.

I think I can make this work. I can follow directions. I can work my tail end off. The predominant way wealth is built in this country is by owning real estate.

Most of us have not seen wealth and the creation of wealth in our families or in our communities. We haven't been taught how to create wealth or had someone who can personally teach us how it's made. We can look at other people and see that they have wealth, but some of us haven't been taught how. We've been left to figure it out. Okay, there's nothing wrong with that, but I was lucky.

MY UNCLE OWNED REAL ESTATE... HE TOLD ME HE DIDN'T NEED A JOB AND THE REASON WHY HE DIDN'T WAS BECAUSE HE OWNED REAL ESTATE

I had an uncle who was my mentor when I was a teenager. He was rich, but I didn't know it. It was something about him that was different than all my family members, and I gravitated to him for some reason. We're sitting around, and I said, "Oh, uncle, what do you do for a job?" He was just a guy who wore Levi's and a tee-shirt and drove a raggedy van. You wouldn't know he was a millionaire.

I said, "Uncle, what do you do for a job? What do you do for work?" He says, "I don't have a job. I own real estate." So as a teenager, I'm going, "What the hell is real estate? I don't know what real estate is. Well, okay, tell me a little bit more."

He says, "I own a duplex. I live on one side. The tenants live on the other side. They pay my rent, my mortgage, my expenses, my clothes, my car." I said, "What?"

He said, "Son, look here. Pay attention. I live on one side. The tenant lives on the other side. They pay for all of my expenses. That's the reason I don't need a job. What I want you to do is to save your money. I want you to buy a house, and I want you to pay it off. Save your money, buy a house, pay it off."

Best advice I've ever received in my whole life. Can you see why I'm debt-free now? It was because of my uncle's advice. It didn't go that easy because I lost two houses to foreclosure in this process, and then on the second foreclosure, I said, "You know what? I'm tired of the banks taking my real estate empire. Once I try to build something up, then in a recession, I lose it, and I get wiped out."

So, I decided I was going to do what my uncle told me to do. My uncle told me to save my money, buy a house and pay it off. That's why I'm debt-free now. Again, see the value of a mentor, you guys?

DEBT IS DANGEROUS… DEBT HAS TO BE PAID BACK WITH INTEREST, AND DEBT DOESN'T EQUAL WEALTH

Just those words, save your money, buy a house, pay it off, have allowed me to be financially free. Most people will tell you to go out and leverage, borrow, borrow, borrow, borrow, borrow. I'm not saying they're wrong, but guess what? Debt is dangerous. Debt has to be paid back with interest. Debt doesn't equal wealth!

I've been through three recessions. In 2001, the 9/11 bombings; 2008, the Great Recession; 2020, COVID. Guess what? COVID didn't affect me at all, because I kept my cash flow. COVID didn't upset my cart, because I did not have any debt on that property, and I still had cash flow.

I'm going to give you a bit of advice right here. If you're out doing real estate, be careful of debt because another recession is coming, and all that hard work you put in, if you're over- leveraged on your real estate, you will lose.

During the 2008 Great Recession, many investors were over-leveraged. Property values dropped, and what happened? Bam, went out of business... this was maybe you?

You may be recovering right now, but guess what? If you start buying real estate without using banks and without using realtors, start doing the unconventional stuff, you can get right back into the game immediately starting today.

Let's talk about the house that I was given for free. It was given to me by an owner who didn't want their property anymore. That property increased my net worth by $1 million dollars, and I did it without money. I did it without credit. I did it without realtors, and I did not have to deal with any banks.

I'm going to talk about money, investing, real estate, building wealth, estate planning, and debt-free living, and we are going to use the calculator. You cannot be an investor if you're not using your calculator to run your numbers.

If you do, you're using your emotions to make investment decisions. You're guessing, and it eventually is going to crush you. You must know how to run your numbers to tell if a deal is a good deal or a deal is a bad deal.

HOW TO ANALYZE YOUR REAL ESTATE DEALS BY KNOWING YOUR FINANCIAL NUMBERS (the KPI's)

I mentioned earlier that one of my coaching students made $1.2 million in one hour. Another student made $400,000 in nine months. I want you to write on a piece of paper, which deal is the best deal?

Is the $1.2 million or the $400,000 the best deal? I'm going to show you how to put it in your calculator so that you will know yourself. I'm going to talk about calculating your return on investment.

As real estate investors, we like to grow and make our money multiply. When we multiply our money, we get a return on our investment. To be a great investor you need to know what your return on investment will be for every deal you work on.

The formula for calculating return on investment is you take your profit and divide it by your investment. Please write that down so that you'll have it.

$400,000 PROFIT FROM A $25,000 INVESTMENT... THAT'S A 1600% RETURN ON HER INVESTMENT!

My student Holly made $400,000 in nine months. She bought 18 notes from this bank. She borrowed $100,000 from family and friends to buy all those notes. From the profits of one deal, she was able to pay them back.

She's got $300,000 of profit and 17 more deals that she has in her portfolio from buying these foreclosure properties from banks. Holly paid $25,000 for her coaching program that taught her how to buy notes from banks. You may be saying, "Wow, that's a lot of money," but you have to remember, we're only going to talk about this one deal where she made $400,000.

Holly invested $25,000 into her real estate education, and I was her coach. Here's what I want you to do. Grab your calculator. Again, it's your profit divided by your investment.

Holly's profit was $400,000. Put that in your calculator, please! Put $400,000 in your calculator, and divide it by $25,000, which is the amount Holly invested.

Tap the equal button, and you'll see a 16, but you have to move the decimal places two places to the right or multiply it by a hundred. Your answer should be 1600.

That's a 1600% return for the $25,000 Holly invested in her real estate education. For every dollar she invested in her training, she made $16 in profit as her return. Was that a good investment on her part?

She invested in herself. She learned a wealth-building strategy, took action and implemented it. She went out into the market and increased her net worth $1.5 million by buying that package of notes.

$1.2 MILLION PROFIT FROM A $110,000 INVESTMENT.
THAT'S A 1090% RETURN ON HIS INVESTMENT!

My coaching student Ron made $1.2 million in one hour. He invested $110,000 of his own money. He went to a bank and said, "I want to buy a building that you own." The bank told Ron, "We can't sell it to you because we don't own it, but we will sell you the note."

Guess what Ron did? He went to the internet to find a mentor. He went to YouTube, and guess who he found? That's right. He found me. He said, "Terry, can you train and mentor me on how to buy notes from banks?" I said, "Yes, I will." Ron was already a millionaire. He already owned commercial property. He just needed me to teach him how to buy notes from banks. Ron goes to the bank after I trained him. The bank's foreclosure property, which was a commercial building, was worth $1.3 million. The property was on one acre of land, and the building was 70,000 square feet.

The bank was owed $850,000 for their note. They were asking $300,000. Ron offered $110,000. The bank accepted. Ron now owns the note. He's now the new bank.

Ron went to the owner to work out a solution, but the owner was no longer interested in owning the business or the commercial property. You may ask, "Terry? How do you make money and build wealth from this commercial real estate deal?"

Ron bought the note from the bank, and then the owner gave Ron the deed to the commercial property. From these two things happening, Ron now owns the commercial property for $110,000.

Let's see what Ron's return on his investment is. Ron made $1.2 million. Please put that in your calculator. Divide that by his investment of $110,000. You should have 10.90, but you have to move it two places to the right or multiply the answer by 100.

Ron's return on his investment is 1090%. For every dollar Ron invested, he profited $10.90. You may say, "So, Terry, tell me about that house that generated a $1 million net worth for you. Tell us about that property that you were given for free that you didn't need a realtor, qualify for any loans or borrow money from banks. You didn't have to use any of your own money, and you didn't have to use your credit?"

$1 MILLION DOLLARS OF GENERATIONAL WEALTH FROM A HOUSE THAT WAS GIVEN TO ME FOR FREE (part 1)

I bought this property for $64,000 in 1999. The first month I bought this property, I made $640 a month in passive cash flow. I have another property that I've owned since 1983. The values of the properties that I own just keep going up, and up, and up. That's how I'm able to build generational wealth for me and my family.

I could sell those houses, but I don't because I don't need the money. I have enough cash flow coming in each and every from my rentals. I'm holding my properties forever and ever. They're the golden goose that keeps producing profits every month. Passive income is the holy grail of real estate, which keeps producing month, after month, after month, after month, and the property goes up, and up, and up. The property is worth $600,000. I have $2,100 a month coming in of positive cash flow. I have no debt on the property.

If someone else could make your house payment for you because you own real estate, would that make you happy? I'm getting $2,100 a month from this rental property. What can $2,100 a month do for you? If somebody else could make your car payment, would that make you happy? If someone else, because you own real estate, would pay for your next family vacation, would that make you happy?

How about if real estate could pay for your kids' or grandkids' college education? If real estate could pay for your house, your car, your vacations, and put your kids through college and still put money in the bank, would that make you happy?

HOW TO BUILD GENERATIONAL WEALTH IN REAL ESTATE WITHOUT QUALIFYING FOR LOANS AND BORROWING MONEY FROM BANKS

This is why I love real estate! I am going to take the average cash flow per year that I've owned the property. I have an average cash flow per month over those 22 years of $1,370. I take $1,370 a month and multiply it by 12. Put those numbers in your calculator. That's $16,440-a-year average.

Take $16,440 and multiply it by 20 years. I've collected $361,680 of estimated rent from this free house that was given to me. I'm going to call it a free house. I'm going to tell you why it's a free house.

$361,680 of rental income that I have coming in plus the $600,000 that this property is worth, that's almost $1 million in net worth. I will never sell this property. Why? Because I want to build generational wealth that I can pass down to my family.

That's why you buy and hold long-term as a real estate investor. Hold some of your real estate for yourself instead of flipping everything so you can have some wealth in the future.

Let me show you the $1 million one more time. I have $361,680 over 22 years of holding this property. It's worth $600,000, that's $961,680, almost $1 million. I didn't need to have any credit, money, a job, or a real estate license. I didn't need a banker's permission to qualify for a loan or borrow money from a bank. I didn't need a pre-qualification letter from a realtor to buy this property.

That's how you build generational wealth. I have this property in my revocable living trust. If you didn't have to go to work at a job because you don't need to work for money anymore, what would you do with your life?

In order to build wealth, you have to know how it's done. Most of us, I'm not saying all of us, have never learned how to build wealth. Our family members were not wealthy. They didn't have real estate in their investment portfolio.

They didn't have businesses. Their families and their parents didn't hand down wealth, like me. I love my mom and dad. They made me who I am. They worked at a job and did the best they could financially. I paid off my real estate before my parents did because of my uncle Austin's advice, which was to buy a house and pay it off.

All my family members, cousins, nieces, nephews, uncles, aunts, my friends, everybody, 99% of the people I knew went to a job except for my uncle Austin.

I can still hear him saying, "Terry, save your money, buy a house, and pay it off!" I'm practically in tears right now because he saved me. He saved me from going to a dead-end job that I didn't like, looking for a watch when I retired.

Now again, you guys, if you have a job, please, I'm not trying to talk down to you, but I just knew I had a different mind when I was growing up. I wanted to be the boss, the entrepreneur, the shot caller, the owner. I wanted to have equity in a business and real estate.

I wanted to own. I wanted to build an empire. I wanted to own, own, own. My uncle said, "Save your money. Buy a house, pay it off." When I went to that seminar, the guy said, "Hey, buy these loans that banks sometimes sell. Buy the loans on these foreclosure properties, and then the owner may give it to you, and then you'll own the house." He was absolutely right! Homeowners facing foreclosure will give you their homes for free because they don't want them.

I had never heard that before. I will tell you this right now – 99% of the people don't know anything about what I'm talking about as far as making money and building wealth being the bank. Everybody wants to be a wholesaler. Everybody wants to fix up the property and flip it. They have to make a reality real estate show about what it takes to be the bank.

I own notes, and I buy them from banks that have properties in foreclosure. Homeowners make their monthly payments to me instead of Bank of America, Wells Fargo, or Chase. I have the same rights that those big banks have. I'm a foreclosure expert. This is what I've been doing since 2001. I'm the number one bank foreclosure mentor in the United States.

Let me tell you about how I got the free house. I couldn't pay for my daughter's college education, and when she said, "Daddy, I want to go to Arizona State University." I felt like a failure because I didn't have the money. I used to own a couple of karate schools. I loved karate. I really thought I was the next Bruce Lee, but it didn't work out that way. I had two karate schools I had opened up.

I'm going to tell you about my third mentor. His name is Carl Dexter. I was living the American dream, I thought, because I owned two karate schools. I was an entrepreneur living the America dream. I owned my own business, but I didn't have any money.

I decided to shut the school down because I wasn't making any money. A good friend of mine that I went to school with was a real estate investor. I knew he was really successful, but I didn't know how successful he was. His daughter was in my karate class. He said, "Terry, you can teach out of my garage for your last few students. My daughter loves you as a karate instructor."

I have a fourth-degree black belt in Taekwondo and a first-degree in Kenpo karate. I spent years and years in martial arts. The first day I went to his house, I was driving, and it seemed like I went from the lower-income neighborhood where I lived to the middle-income neighborhood, then all of a sudden, it started being the upper real estate neighborhood of my city.

I'm like, "Wait a minute. I must be going in the wrong direction!" As I kept going, I pulled up in front of Carl's house. Carl has this big, beautiful, two-story home in a gorgeous gated community. A guy that I went to school with, a guy that I grew up with. I'm jealous. I'm going to just be honest with you guys. I'm jealous of where Carl is living. How is he living here when I'm living in the lower-priced neighborhood?

So, I asked Carl how he got this house. He told me, "I bought the house from the developer that went bankrupt. Carl showed me check, after check, after check, after check, after check, after check, after check that he had made investing in real estate. I'm like, "Whoa. I got a new mentor." I said, "Hey, man, you got to teach me. I'm up against it financially. What did you do to make all this money?"

He said, "Terry, I started knocking on the doors of homeowners in foreclosure." He was a door knocker. I said, "That's what I'm going to do, sun up to sundown. I'm going to knock on the doors of homeowners facing foreclosure so I can be financially successful in real estate."

It was either get rich or die trying for me, because I had nothing to lose. My daughter was ready for college. I had no money. I was teaching karate classes because I had no money. I had a dead-end job that I didn't like. All that was working against me. I was in the struggle.

So, if you're in a financial struggle, please listen to me. You can do this real estate if you're in the struggle. So, what did I do, you guys? All day, all night I was knocking on the doors of homeowners facing foreclosure. I went to this $600,000 house and knocked on the door.

Pay attention. This is how I got this house for free. I knock on the door and I ask, "Hey, is John there? The lady says, "John just passed away." I said, "Sorry to hear that John passed away. What are you going to do with that property that's in foreclosure?" She told me she was going to give it back to the bank.

John was the real estate guy. I only want to spend time with my grandkids. I said, "I'd like to have the property. Can I have the property that has two houses on it?" She says, "Terry, I'll give them to you." She didn't ask me for any money. If I wouldn't have taken those houses, they would have gone back to the bank as a foreclosure. She didn't care about those houses because she was a grieving widow. She didn't like real estate. Her grandkids were more important than real estate or rent money.

Can you guys understand why she gave me that property for free? She wasn't emotionally tied to the property. She gave me the houses for free because they had no value to her. I've been given at least 10 free houses from people because they didn't want them.

If you don't know anything about this, you will not know what I'm talking about. You would never, ever be able to do it unless someone like me shows you how it's done. I've been doing real estate like this for the last 21 years of my life.

The property was $8,000 behind on payments. I borrowed the $8,000 from my dad. I didn't have any money. I didn't have the credit. It was owed $64,000 in 1999 and the loan on that property was a VA loan that anybody could assume regardless of their credit score. With that being said, I didn't need to qualify for any bank loans to own that property.

If I had gone to a realtor and told them I was interested in buying this house, what would they have said? "Terry, you need a pre-qualification letter." So that means going to the bank and getting a loan. I wouldn't have qualified.

The $1 million that this property is worth is going to generate income for life for me and my family. Realtors and bankers would've denied me the dream, because I wasn't a traditional buyer. This is America. Everybody deserves to be able to live the American dream.

We all deserve to be wealthy with zero barriers, regardless of our credit score and what we have or don't have in our bank account. If you're renting right now, you can own a home for you and your family. The house that the lady gave to me – you can do that, too, but you need me to coach and train you how to do it. I am an expert at dealing with people in foreclosure. Here's a picture of the houses after I remodeled them both. As of 9/2023, the property rents for $4,138 a month.

You Will Work For Someone Else
The Rest of Your Life
If You Don't Become
A Student of Investing!

Click the link below or scan the QR code to view video
https://www.youtube.com/watch?v=Vz7UwOrmE4A

I rehabbed this property in the hopes of selling it. I had two buyers fall out of escrow, so I decided to keep it and rent it.

Here are the videos of the property transformation. Click the links or scan the QR code so you can see first-hand what it took for me to remodel two houses. It took me a total of 107 days from start to finish to complete the rehab.

200' fence replacement
https://www.youtube.com/watch?v=2YPnjRk6s7M

Replacing old siding (1)
https://www.youtube.com/watch?v=7rxGjh3HRVY

Replacing old siding (2)
https://www.youtube.com/watch?v=YuUPI57gDmM

Replacing old siding (3)
https://www.youtube.com/watch?v=lbS2TEFAZz4

Insulating the house
https://www.youtube.com/watch?v=iOBunbkP9tI

New siding installation (1)
https://www.youtube.com/watch?v=deHQoWdbcao

New siding installation (2)
https://www.youtube.com/watch?v=tt4onx4hlC8

New siding installation (3)
https://www.youtube.com/watch?v=SqCEjVd9qrY

Dump run
https://www.youtube.com/watch?v=eIrf-Qe4Bug

Second house backyard (1)
https://www.youtube.com/watch?v=elTCb-5QY-8

Second house backyard (2)
https://www.youtube.com/watch?v=Bb-Y1zw82dc

Working on Sunday
https://www.youtube.com/watch?v=t6wsfK8VI8k

Ready to start fencing
https://www.youtube.com/watch?v=fOs5U-YHxcQ

Fencing finished
https://www.youtube.com/watch?v=_HHYLAWQ5kI

16 yards of gravel
https://www.youtube.com/watch?v=JbAo08Jc8jc

Roof tear off
https://www.youtube.com/watch?v=leef8lmZ91w

Ready for new roofing
https://www.youtube.com/watch?v=d7aLW8B0WH8

Rick's shooting the video for MLS
https://www.youtube.com/watch?v=2c1-pkBjrpI

Carport painted- roofing finished
https://www.youtube.com/watch?v=uBdExRnGo_0

New sod and concrete sidewalk
https://www.youtube.com/watch?v=GrGbwtr_EXg

Staging exterior – looking for buyer
https://www.youtube.com/watch?v=cYOG5bgctwE

Interior demo (1)
https://www.youtube.com/watch?v=h0dqbBkDFus

Interior demo (2)
https://www.youtube.com/watch?v=S88Fhto-f1c

Laminate flooring installed
https://www.youtube.com/watch?v=tsn_tH8MK-s

Fumigation
https://www.youtube.com/watch?v=yu6WDTqwnA4

Prepping bathroom
https://www.youtube.com/watch?v=tsnKgvTLhY0

Shaker cabinets delivered
https://www.youtube.com/watch?v=auTgTByqJ-U

Bathroom almost finished
https://www.youtube.com/watch?v=38VlkWncA6I

Ready for buyer inspection
https://www.youtube.com/watch?v=nrm7ucsuU48

Front house is finished
https://www.youtube.com/watch?v=pvhaeHYDhUI

Back house ready for rehab
https://www.youtube.com/watch?v=SStPzx_LRns

Back house is finished
https://www.youtube.com/watch?v=Q6sA6ZBTn0E

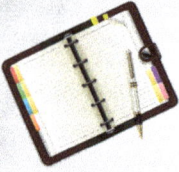

Wealth For The Rest Of Us *is the battle cry of the middle class, the poor, minorities and marginalized communities.*

It's the manifesto of those struggling with their finances. Those struggling with getting more out of their situation. Those fighting for their right to provide for their loved ones.

WEALTH FOR THE REST OF US REPRESENTS THAT FIGHT!

—Terry Bontemps

What Terry Bontemps Hopes You Learn From Reading His Book "Wealth For The Rest Of Us"

WE ALL SHOULD BE WEALTHY... Real estate investment has historically been the pathway to building wealth for many Americans. This is evident in the book "Wealth For The Rest Of Us", which highlights the teachings and strategies of Terry Bontemps, financial educator, author, wealth teacher and bank note buying expert. Terry emphasizes the importance of real estate as a means of creating wealth and achieving financial success.

1. **Homeownership As A Source Of Wealth Creation**: *Wealth For The Rest of Us* starts by stating that homeownership is the principal source of wealth creation for most people. This is a widely accepted belief and is supported by data and research. Owning a home allows individuals to build equity over time, which can be a significant asset and source of wealth.

2. **Buying Notes From Banks As An Investment Vehicle:** Terry Bontemps emphasizes that when people think about real estate, they often focus on the physical structure (the house which is owned by the seller) rather than the financial aspect (the note which is owned by the bank). Terry encourages individuals to shift their mindset from being flippers & landlords to recognizing the potential for wealth creation through owning the note and becoming the bank.

3. **Key Performance Indicators (10 KPIs):** Terry Bontemps introduces the concept of KPIs in real estate investing. These are metrics and data points that help investors evaluate the profitability and potential risk of loss on a real estate deal. The KPIs mentioned in *Wealth For The Rest of Us* include total profit, total investment, return on investment, time to get investment back, payback period, profit margin %, equity, buying real estate on the dollar, for every dollar you invest, how much in return you'll make plus multiplied

and increased investment. By analyzing these 10 KPIs, investors can make informed financial decisions and identify profitable investment opportunities.

4. **Case Studies And Examples**: *Wealth For The Rest of Us* provides several case studies and examples to illustrate the potential for wealth creation through real estate investing. These examples include individuals who have made significant profits by buying notes, foreclosures, commercial properties, and distressed properties. The document highlights the high returns on investment, profit margins, and multiples of money that can be achieved through strategic real estate investments.

5. **Overcoming Common Challenges**: Terry Bontemps addresses common challenges and misconceptions about real estate investing. He dispels myths such as the need for large amounts of money, good credit, or previous experience to invest in real estate. He emphasizes that anyone can invest in real estate and achieve financial success with the right knowledge, strategy, and mentorship.

6. **Real Estate Education And Training**: Terry Bontemps promotes his mobile app, Bank Foreclosure Millionaire, as a resource for individuals to learn how to invest in real estate and build wealth. The app offers educational materials, training programs, and a real estate investment game to help individuals develop the necessary skills and knowledge to succeed in real estate. Terry Bontemps wants to take the complicated world of learning real estate and make it easy for anyone to understand so they can pass generational wealth down to their family.

7. **The Importance of Financial Education**: Throughout *Wealth For The Rest of Us*, Terry Bontemps emphasizes the importance of financial education in achieving wealth and

financial success. He encourages individuals to educate themselves about money, finance, and investing, particularly in the context of real estate. By understanding key financial principles and strategies, individuals can make informed decisions and take control of their financial future. No matter the financial struggles you've experienced or what stage you're currently on with your financial journey, you will grow an appreciation for money, personal finance and financial literacy from reading this book.

8. **The Role of Mentors**: *Wealth For The Rest of Us* emphasizes the importance of having a mentor in real estate investment. It highlights the success story of Terry Bontemps who has been mentored by experienced investors and how he has achieved significant financial gains as a result. Having a mentor can provide guidance, knowledge, and support by helping you navigate the complexities of real estate investment and avoid common pitfalls.

9. **Overcome Financial Limitations**: Focus on acquiring the necessary knowledge, education, and experience to make money in real estate without relying solely on your own personal funds, credit and experience as the reasons stopping your from investing in real estate.

10. **Develop A Money Mindset and Financial Freedom Goals**: Shift from working for a paycheck to building wealth. Envision how your life would change if you were financially free. Your goal should be to get the point where you don't have to work anymore for money, that's the definition of being "wealthy" then you can start living your personal mission every day of your life. Use real estate to pay off your debt, save, invest, multiply your money and build generational wealth.

11. **Take Action and Implement Terry Bontemps Investment Strategies**: Apply the knowledge gained from the book and Terry's teachings, actively seek opportunities, and start investing in real estate. Start buying real estate to hold for long term wealth or to flip for quick cash profits. Make real estate your side hustle and the vehicle that makes you wealthy.

In conclusion, real estate investment has historically been a proven pathway to building wealth for many Americans. Through strategic investments, individuals can generate significant profits, build equity, and achieve financial success. *Wealth For The Rest of Us* highlights the teachings and strategies of Terry Bontemps, a wealth teacher and real estate investor, who emphasizes the importance of real estate as a means of creating wealth and achieving financial freedom.

DISRUPT

THE BANKING INDUSTRY: BANKS DICTATE BEHAVIOR

ALL BANKS KEEP DOING IS CREATING NEW WAYS TO KEEP YOU IN DEBT.
THEY TRY TO OWN & CONTROL YOU, YOUR FAMILY AND YOUR MONEY,
BY GIVING YOU NOTES ATTACHED TO PROPERTY AND THINGS YOU THINK
YOU OWN. MOST PEOPLE AVOID THE NOTE, NEVER REALIZING THE NOTE
IS WHAT BANKS HAVE USED TO ENSLAVE THEM FINANCIALLY

The statis quo is the current state of things. If you are already wealthy,
then you're most likely not interested in disrupting the status quo...

CHAPTER 1:

THE BEST FINANCIAL ADVICE

I'VE EVER RECEIVED IN MY LIFE

WEALTH HABIT #1: BEING DEBT-FREE

My uncle's advice was for me to save my money, buy a house and pay it off. I'm glad I listened to him, because today I have no debt on the real estate that I own or my home. I don't have any credit card debt, student loan debt, automobile debt, or any other debt. I'm my own bank! I don't pay interest to banks. I pay cash for everything. The reason I'm able to do this is because I listened to my uncle, invested in real estate and paid off my debt… because of his advice, I no longer have to work for money!

—Terry Bontemps

I had a mentor in my teenage years, my uncle, who was a real estate investor. When I was 20 years old, I followed my wealthy uncle's valuable advice, which was to save money, buy a house, and then pay it off. I ended up losing my first house and another house to foreclosure, but I'm glad I listened to him and his advice.

One day, I questioned him about his job. He said, "I don't have a job. I'm a real estate investor. I buy and own real estate. I work for myself, and I'm my own boss. I own a duplex. I live on one side; the tenant lives on the other side. The tenant pays all of my expenses to live. The tenant pays for all my expenses. The tenant pays the mortgage on my property. The tenant pays for the living expenses for me to live on, because I'm the landlord. I don't need a job, because I own real estate."

I asked, "What did you say? My mom, dad, uncle, nieces, aunts, friends, and in-laws all have jobs, and they work for money… a paycheck. So, wait a minute. Don't you have a job?"

SO, HOW DO YOU MAKE MONEY? HOW DO YOU MAKE A LIVING? I'M A REAL ESTATE INVESTOR!

"How does that work again?" He said, "Look, son, pay attention. This property that I own is a duplex. I live on one side, and on the other side lives the tenant. The tenant pays all of my expenses. They pay for the mortgage on the property. They pay all my expenses; they pay for my food. They pay for my groceries, my clothes, my car, living expenses, everything from the rent I charge them."

"What? You don't need to have a job or need to work for a boss because you own real estate... this duplex?"

He goes, "Yeah. Let me tell you something. You buy yourself some real estate, maybe a duplex like I have. You need to save your money so you can buy real estate, and I would be grateful if you could pay it off so you don't have any debt."

As a teenager, he taught me what the rich teach their children about owning real estate and building wealth... He told me not to blow my money. He wanted me to pay off my real estate so I wouldn't have any debt. He told me that debt doesn't equal wealth. Debt is what keeps most people from having any real wealth. It's the best advice I've ever received in my life!

WHY?

Because today, I don't owe banks any money! I owe banks no money on the real estate that I own. I have no debt, no credit card debt, no automobile debt, and no student loan debt. I don't owe anybody money. I pay all cash when I buy... I haven't checked my credit score or used credit, probably in the last 20 years. I don't depend on banks.

I am my own bank. I bank on myself to remain financially free. I took the profits I made from my real estate deals to pay off my debt, including my automobiles, home, and rental properties.

I don't even use credit. I don't have a credit score from me not using credit. I don't depend on banks. I bank on myself so that I can remain financially free. The hundreds of thousands of dollars in interest you're paying to banks is the money you need to survive and live a better life for you and your family. People have become so dependent on banks. My uncle taught me how to be my own bank. How many people ever become their own bank?

How many people ever pay themselves first by becoming their own bank? The No. 1 financial strategy, bar none, for building wealth is you becoming your own bank. We have yet to be formally taught how to be our bank, paying ourselves instead of paying the bank. In Monopoly, the bank controls the game and makes the rules. The bank controls the board game, financial institutions, properties, houses, and motels, which is how it works in real life.

Banks can help you build wealth, which is great. Banks also can keep you broke, in debt, and from having generational wealth... Banks are constantly creating new ways to keep you, your family, and your friends broke. You can invest and build wealth in real estate without using banks. You can finance yourself on your next home purchase without borrowing money and getting loans from banks!

Imagine starting from nothing and accumulating more money, generational wealth, and real estate than you ever thought possible for you and your family. Imagine one day being in a position where you no longer need to work for a living. Wealth, to me, is when you one day get to the point where you don't have to work for money anymore. Perhaps you want to quit your job, spend more time with your loved ones, or travel to destinations you've never imagined. Maybe you want to give to charities that have a significant influence. For some, we want to finally live the life that we truly deserve, free from debt and the pressure of scarcity. The American dream is about anyone being able to start from nothing, nada, zilch, much like immigrants who come to this country and go on to make their fortunes investing, buying, and owning real estate.

This book and my mobile app, Bank Foreclosure Millionaire, will show you step-by-step "exactly" how I got started investing in real estate without money, credit, a real estate license, a job, a pre-qualification letter, and without getting loans from banks. Fortunately, you can succeed investing in real estate, make money, and build wealth too, because real estate is an equal opportunity wealth builder.

This book and my mobile app, Bank Foreclosure Millionaire, is a step-by-step guide for anyone wanting to acquire wealth. I will teach you how to acquire wealth, multiply your wealth, protect your wealth and be able to pass wealth down using my investment strategies. The best feature is that practically anyone can make real estate investments and achieve financial freedom. My life and financial security didn't significantly alter until I began investing in real estate. Anyone can get wealthy!

Building wealth is a habit. Building wealth never stops, and you should be getting a return on your investment every day.

OWNING A HOME IS A SAVVY FINANCIAL MOVE

For most families, their home purchase will be the largest financial purchase of their life. As their home value increases, so does their net worth. Renters don't gain the advantage that homeowners do with regard to net worth from the increase in equity. The renter's landlord increases their net worth when property values rise.

Owning a home will save you from 30 years or more of renting. If you're renting at $1,500 a month, that's $18,000 a year. After renting for 30 years, that $540,000 goes to your landlord. Imagine a half million dollars gone that could have made you and your family wealthy instead of your landlord. And, you have no ownership and nothing to show for that half-a-million dollars either that you've spent on rent. Overall, home prices will continually rise, but they occasionally go down. Paying off your home early, like I did on all of my real estate holdings, can result in earning you a nice return on your investment. It will also add monthly passive income to the bottom line of your bank account. One of my coaching students made an 18% return on her investment and banked an extra $900 a month by paying her $60,000 mortgage off early. She invested in her debt and paid off her home. Keeping money in the bank would have earned her 1%, 2%, or maybe 3%, which is not great. Her stock investments couldn't match the 18% return on her investment made by paying off her mortgage. She became her own bank by paying off her mortgage. She paid herself instead of paying the bank, and that's smart financially.

Everybody has to live somewhere, which makes buying a home a great investment. The average person is accustomed to spending up to a third or more of their income on housing. You might as well spend that third on ownership. Over time, more people have achieved an increase in their net worth due to owning their home.

My uncle told me to save my money, buy a house and pay it off. After spending the last 42 years in real estate and owning my properties free and clear, here's what I've learned. My home is an asset, not a liability, regardless of what the so-called experts are saying. I recommend you buy a home and pay it off. Why? Because 30 years goes by really fast. I have a comfortable place to live, and I own it free and clear. I only have to pay property taxes, which amounts to $200 a month. I've owned this property since 1980. It's going to be passed down to my daughters for generational wealth. I don't have the financial burden of a high mortgage or high rent, plus I've saved thousands and thousands of dollars of interest that I would have normally paid to the bank by financing the property. I'm the bank… I pay myself first. This is how I've become my own bank, and I hope you do the same!

Click the link below or scan the QR code to view video
https://www.youtube.com/watch?v=1EDmdkHOBOE&t=15s

Most people live the 40-40-40 life, that's 40 hours a week for 40 years of their life, and then retire with a 40% pay cut called Social Security.

The 5 Millionaire Habits That Made Me Wealthy:

1. Being debt free
2. Having a revocable living trust
3. Being my own bank
4. Knowing how to multiply my money
5. Owning real estate

Learn how to make money, build wealth, and be a real estate millionaire. Teach your kids and teens about money, finance, and investing. Download Terry's mobile app Bank Foreclosure Millionaire from Amazon or Apple Store today, $19.99.

Chapter 1 Takeaways and Actionable Steps For You To Take

Chapter 1: Discusses the importance of being debt-free as the best financial advice Terry Bontemps has ever received. Terry's uncle advised him to save his money, buy a house, and pay it off. Here are the key takeaways from this chapter and actionable items for the reader:

1. **Debt-Free Living**: The chapter emphasizes the importance of living a debt-free life. Being debt-free allows individuals to have more financial freedom, flexibility and not be indebted to banks and financial institutions.

2. **Save Money**: The author's uncle advised him to save his money. This is a crucial step in achieving financial stability and being able to make significant purchases without relying on credit. When you don't have debt, you can save money.

3. **Buy A House**: The author's uncle recommended buying a house as a long-term investment. Owning a home can provide stability and potential appreciation in value over time. Owning a home makes you wealthy instead making your landlord wealthy.

4. **Pay Off The House**: The author's uncle emphasized the importance of paying off the mortgage on the house. This eliminates a significant monthly expense and allows individuals to build equity in their home. Not having a mortgage payment allows you to save that monthly payment that you can deposit in your bank account or invest with.

Actionable items for the reader:

1. **Create A Budget**: Start by creating a budget to track income and expenses. This will help identify areas where money can be saved and put towards debt repayment or savings.

2. **Save Regularly**: Set aside a portion of your passive cash flow for savings. Invest that savings to multiply your money. Take that money and pay off debt. Get to the point where you don't have to work for money anymore which is Terry's definition of being wealthy. Take the profits from buying, selling, flipping and managing your real estate portfolio to pay off your debt faster.

3. **Prioritize Debt Repayment**: Make a plan to pay off any outstanding debts, starting with paying off the debt that will return you the high-interest rate return. By paying off the debt with the highest return will put more money in your pocket each and every month & allow you to payoff low-interest rate return debt faster. Take the profits from buying, selling, flipping and managing your real estate portfolio to pay off your debt faster.

4. **Consider Homeownership**: Evaluate your financial situation and determine if homeownership is a viable option for you. Terry recommends buying a home and paying it off as fast as you can. When you're 30 years older (which goes by really fast), you will have a comfortable paid off home with no mortgage payment to a bank or rent payment to make to a landlord. This was the advice Terry's uncle gave him when he was a teenager. Best advice Terry's ever received. It's the reason Terry's debt free today and why he doesn't have to work for money another day in his life which is his definition of being wealthy.

5. **Create A Mortgage Payoff Plan**: If you already own a home, develop a plan to pay off your mortgage early. Consider making extra principal payments. It's amazing to see how much interest can be saved by removing 15 years of interest payments!

6. **Seek Financial Advice**: Consult with a financial advisor or real estate professional to get personalized advice and guidance on your specific financial situation and goals.

Remember, achieving financial freedom and being debt-free is a journey that requires discipline, patience, and consistent effort. By following these actionable steps, you can start taking control of your finances and work towards a debt-free future.

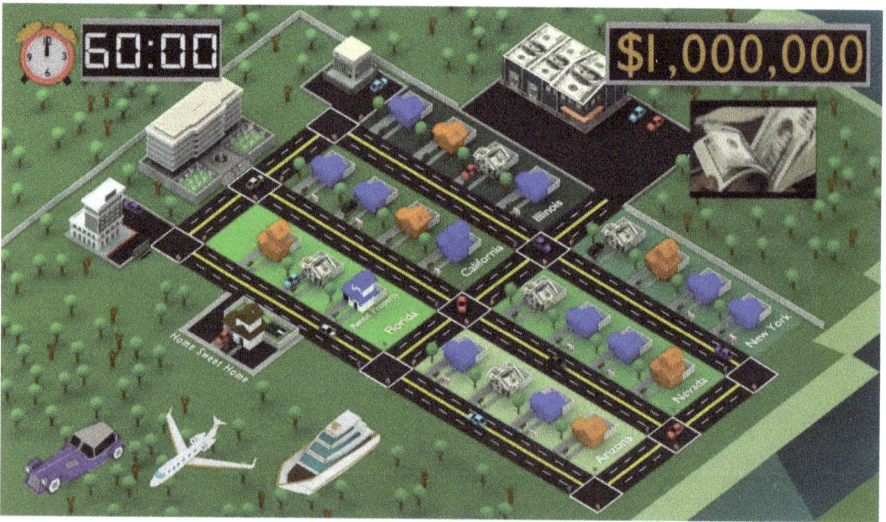

CHAPTER 2:
HERE'S HOW IMPORTANT OWNING REAL ESTATE IS TO BUILDING GENERATIONAL WEALTH

WEALTH HABIT #2: HAVING A REVOCABLE TRUST

**PLEASE GOOGLE AND READ
"WHEN MY MOTHER DIED WITHOUT A WILL,
I LEARNED A BIG LESSON ABOUT MONEY
MANAGEMENT AS AN AFRICAN AMERICAN,"
WRITTEN BY ANGIE CHATMAN**

I bought a foreclosure property for $64,000 in 1999. I rented it for $1,200. In 2021, it was worth $600,000, and I rented it for $2,100 a month. As of today, 2023, the property is rented for $4,100 a month... I have no debt on the property. There is no mortgage. I own it free and clear. I am my own bank...

The monthly rent has increased 341% in the 24 years that I've owned the property. This foreclosure property was given to me by the owner for FREE.

The owner didn't ask me for any money. I didn't have to get a loan or borrow any money from a bank. I didn't work with realtors, and I didn't need any credit, a job, or a real estate license. Almost $1 million dollars has been added to my net worth due to this one property that I'll be passing down in generational wealth to my daughters.

—Terry Bontemps

HERE'S HOW IMPORTANT OWNING REAL ESTATE IS TO BUILDING GENERATIONAL WEALTH

Bruce's Beach

In 1912, there was an African-American family that owned beachfront property in Manhattan Beach, California. The property was called Bruce's Beach. It was owned by Charles and Willa Bruce.

In 1924 the Manhattan Beach City Council decided to unjustly take the property from the Bruce Family by eminent domain. They did it to drive out a successful Black-owned businesses. The Bruces would have been multi-millionaires if they would have been allowed to keep their property. Today, that land is valued to be worth $20 million.

After 98 years, the Los Angeles County Board of Supervisors rightfully returned the land to the legal heirs of Charles and Willa Bruce with restitution. They will lease the property from the heirs at $400,000 a year and then purchase the property for no more than $20 million.

Here's a great 65-minute video of Bruce's Beach dedication ceremony and celebration by the Los Angeles County Board of Supervisors.

Click the link below or scan the QR code to view video
https://www.youtube.com/watch?v=kzTW95o7l5E

HERE'S HOW IMPORTANT OWNING REAL ESTATE IS TO BUILDING GENERATIONAL WEALTH

George Nolfi (Director of *The Banker* movie)

I think it's important for people to understand that the main way that Americans build wealth is by property ownership. If a whole group of American people are denied the ability to acquire a home because they can't get loans in certain neighborhoods, then it becomes very hard to build generational wealth and pass wealth down.

I just think it's something not understood by a lot of people, so I hope *The Banker* movie, in a very fun way, allows people to see that issue. The banker tells the story of an important piece of Black history, and it seems inspired by true events. This central story of the film, as we said, is largely unknown. Why do you think that it's taken so long to hear the story, and how does it feel to be telling it now?

I'm, you know, incredibly thankful for the opportunity to tell this story. As you said, it's been out there for a long time. I think because of the nature of the story in the 50s and 60s. The incredible feats that they did prior to when the government really focused on them were not really reported on. There was a little bit in *Ebony* and *Jet* magazines, but there wasn't much in the, you know, quote-unquote mainstream white press. So, the story just disappeared, and these guys kind of got erased from history, and so I'm glad that society has moved on to a place where we can dig this story up.

The Banker is obviously an entertaining movie about a group of folks who defied the odds and beat the system that had been stacked against them. Here's a great seven-minute video of George Nolfi's interview discussing *The Banker* movie

Click the link below or scan the QR code to view the video
https://www.youtube.com/watch?v=T5PUz0dy6Ew&t=268s

HERE'S HOW IMPORTANT OWNING REAL ESTATE IS TO BUILDING GENERATIONAL WEALTH

The Banker movie

It is a true-life story about Joe Morris and Bernard Garrett, two of the first African- Americans in the United States to build real estate and banking empires. Joe Morris is played by Samuel Jackson, and Bernard Garrett is played by Anthony Mackie. The movie is about real estate, business, entrepreneurship, and banking.

It's an inspirational, positive, and encouraging movie about two successful real estate tycoons in Los Angeles who acquired real estate holdings all over California, Texas, and the Bahamas. Together, in 1963, they bought the Bankers building, a 13-story building, which was the largest and tallest commercial building in downtown Los Angeles.

Garrett and Morris built a real estate and banking portfolio worth tens of millions of dollars, which equates to well over $100 million in today's dollars. They owned a large boat marina and resort in the Bahamas. They owned two ranches in Barstow, California. They owned four to five banks, savings and loans, mortgage, and finance companies in Texas. They owned commercial and residential real estate totaling more than 170 buildings and parcels of land when it was virtually illegal for anyone Black to do so.

In 1926, Morris was worth over $2 million with offices in New York, San Francisco, and Beverly Hills. Garrett had achieved a net worth of $1.5 million.

The reason they bought banks was to positively impact their neighborhoods and to provide loans and economic opportunities to other African Americans for purchasing businesses and real estate, which had been previously shut out of the banking system. They did these things during the 1960s, so they had to figure out a way to overcome systematic racism and housing discrimination to be financially successful. These two men were very instrumental in developing the Fair Housing Act of 1968.

The movie sheds light on how systematic racism, particularly in the banking and housing market, shows how African Americans were held back from owning homes. If you can't get a loan to own a home, then it becomes extremely hard to build generational wealth and pass wealth down. The predominant way wealth is built in this country or any other country is by owning real estate. Here's a great 17-minute video overview of *The Banker* movie that has over 22 million views

Click the link below or scan the QR code to view the video
https://www.youtube.com/watch?v=jYvcRZ7QKOU

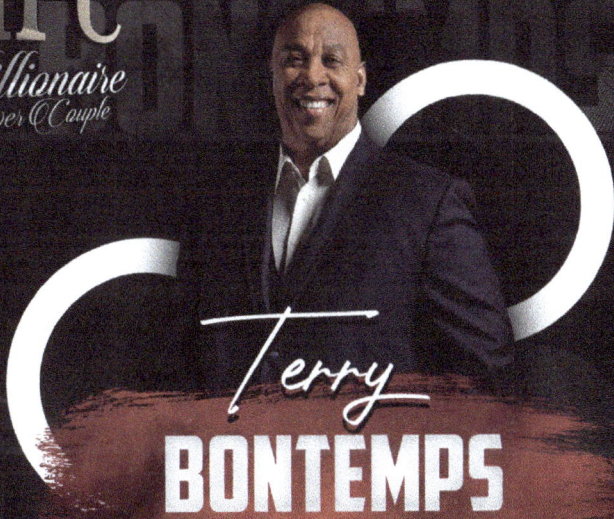

HERE'S HOW IMPORTANT OWNING REAL ESTATE IS TO BUILDING GENERATIONAL WEALTH

$1 Million Dollars of Generational Wealth From a House That Was Given to Me for Free (Part 2)

I knocked on the door of a homeowner who was facing foreclosure. Her husband had recently passed away. She told me that she had no interest in owning the real estate and that she was going to give the property back to the bank.

Her husband was the one who spent a considerable amount of time building their real estate portfolio. All she wanted to do was spend time with her grandchildren.

I asked her if I could have the properties, and she said yes. She didn't ask me for any money. The property was owed $64,000 in 1999, and that's what I bought it for.

The property had two houses on one lot. The mortgage payment was $640 per month.

I rented out the property for $1,000 a month. I made $460 a month passive cash flow. In 2021, I had both properties rented for $2,100 a month. Today, the rent is $4,100 a month.

I have no mortgage on the property. I paid the loan off. I don't owe banks any money. I own it free and clear. The property is in a revocable trust, and I plan on passing the property to my daughters so they can have some wealth and income.

Here's the video of my $1 million dollar profit from a free house.

Click the link or scan the QR code to view.
https://www.youtube.com/watch?v=Tw1-KWQ6hvo

IF YOU CHOOSE TO WORK FOR SOMEONE ELSE YOUR ENTIRE LIFE, YOU HAVE VERY LITTLE CHANCE OF BECOMING FINANCIALLY INDEPENDENT!

Eight Ways to Buy Real Estate With No Money, Credit, Banks, or Realtors

1. Subject-to
2. Wholesaling
3. Money partner
4. Private lender
5. Hard money lender
6. Buy the note
7. Cash for keys
8. Deed in-lieu of foreclosure

Learn how to make money, build wealth, and be a real estate millionaire. Teach your kids and teens about money, finance, and investing. Download Terry's mobile app Bank Foreclosure Millionaire from Amazon or Apple Store today, $19.99.

WHEN YOU INVEST YOUR MONEY, YOU SHOULD KNOW...

1. How much is your profit
2. How much is your investment
3. What's your return on investment
4. Time to get investment back
5. Your profit margin %
6. Equity in the property
7. Buying real estate on the dollar for
8. Multiplied investment by
9. Payback period (based on expected ROI)
10. For every dollar you invest, you will make $_____

—**Terry Bontemps**

Chapter 2 Takeaways and Actionable Steps For You To Take

Chapter 2: Emphasizes the importance of owning real estate in building generational wealth. The key takeaways from this chapter are:

1. **Real Estate As A Wealth-Building Strategy**: The chapter highlights that real estate is a proven and effective way to build wealth over time. It states that owning real estate is crucial for creating generational wealth and leaving a legacy for future generations.

2. **Real Estate As A Source Of Passive Income**: The chapter emphasizes that real estate can provide passive income through note buying, rental properties, Airbnb, and residential assisted living. By investing in rental properties, individuals can generate consistent cash flow that can support their financial goals and provide long-term financial security.

3. **Benefits Of Real Estate Ownership**: The chapter discusses the benefits of owning real estate, such as potential appreciation in property value, tax advantages, and the ability to leverage assets to acquire more properties. It highlights that real estate ownership allows individuals to build equity and create wealth over time.

4. **Real Estate As A Long-Term Investment**: The chapter emphasizes the importance of taking a long-term approach to real estate investing. It states that real estate is not a get-rich-quick scheme, but rather a strategy that requires patience, discipline, and a long-term perspective. It encourages readers to view real estate as a long-term investment that can provide financial stability and growth over time.

5. **Actionable Items For Readers**: The chapter encourages readers to take action by considering real estate as a wealth-building strategy. It suggests that readers educate themselves about real estate investing, seek mentorship or guidance from experienced investors, and start exploring potential investment opportunities. It also mentions the author's mobile app, Bank Foreclosure Millionaire, as a resource for learning about real estate investing.

Overall, the chapter emphasizes the importance of real estate ownership in building generational wealth and provides actionable steps for readers to start their real estate investment journey.

CHAPTER 3: WEALTH
FOR THE REST OF US

DISRUPT
THE BANKING INDUSTRY: BANKS DICTATE BEHAVIOR

ALL BANKS KEEP DOING IS CREATING NEW WAYS TO KEEP YOU IN DEBT.
THEY TRY TO OWN & CONTROL YOU, YOUR FAMILY AND YOUR MONEY,
BY GIVING YOU NOTES ATTACHED TO PROPERTY AND THINGS YOU THINK
YOU OWN. MOST PEOPLE AVOID THE NOTE, NEVER REALIZING THE NOTE
IS WHAT BANKS HAVE USED TO ENSLAVE THEM FINANCIALLY

The statis quo is the current state of things. If you are already wealthy,
then you're most likely not interested in disrupting the status quo...

The reality is nobody's going to get ahead getting paid by the hour. That's living paycheck to paycheck. You have to have equity in something like real estate, a business or intellectual property to have any chance of being wealthy.

—Terry Bontemps

WEALTHY… You want to be wealthy… Your mother wants to be wealthy. Your brother and uncle want to be wealthy, too. Everybody wants to be wealthy… right?

We all have aspirations and dreams of being wealthy, but unless you have a plan, unless you have a strategy… you have absolutely no hope of being wealthy… and so there are some facts that we have to accept.

FACT #1 —YOUR JOB WILL NOT MAKE YOU WEALTHY!

And while that may not feel good to hear, it's still true. Your job will not make you wealthy. Right? You will never earn your way to financial freedom. You don't get wealthy just by working for money… You can't work enough jobs or get enough clients…

WHY? Because the tax man and the interest you pay to banks in interest will take it! You get wealthy by multiplying your money by investing in real estate.

FACT #2 — YOU'RE UNLIKELY TO EVER HIT THE LOTTERY!

FACT #3 — THAT INHERITANCE YOU'RE LOOKING FOR FROM THAT RICH UNCLE, YEAH, THAT'S NEVER GOING TO HAPPEN EITHER!

So, how do you generate wealth coming from the position you are in life? How do you turn your career sacrifices, because that's what you're doing… you're sacrificing your talents, your skill sets, your education, and your labor in order to receive compensation from that place we call our job into prosperity for you and your family?

How do you turn that sacrifice into wealth? How do you turn it into the things that you aspire to have and do? And so, this is why I created this movement called "WEALTH FOR THE REST OF US."

The reality is that, oftentimes, when you look at many of the different wealth-building strategies out there, they automatically exclude most of us… and we feel that exclusion every day, then we have titles.

Basically, there's the wealthy, there's the middle class, and there's the poor. Most of us fall into the bottom two. And they give us a label that immediately lets us know that we are excluded from better opportunities for our families. We are excluded from the ability to live our dreams. We are excluded from traveling. We are excluded. And so I wanted to come up with a plan that made it highly possible and highly likely for regular everyday folks to generate wealth with what they were working with.

My wealth-building game plan is not predicated on you having $1 million in the bank or even $100,000 in your bank account. My wealth-building game plan is not predicated on your credit score, it's based on the understanding of how to use other people's money. It's predicated on how to use real estate strategies in a way that allows you to generate real wealth for you and your family.

So, in this book, I'm going to be talking about "WEALTH FOR THE REST OF US."

Because for far too long, those who don't have wealth have been excluded from having any damn thing. So, at the end of the day, wealth typically excludes the have-nots. Wealth is usually the province of people who already have it, and it rarely allows people who don't to have any damn thing.

Now that being said, "WEALTH FOR THE REST OF US" is my thing. This is my movement and my mission. This is the thing that I'm going to be talking about. A carpenter is a person who builds the houses of others or constructs for others. Right?

Whereas, if all he did was build his own house and all he did was work on his own stuff, we wouldn't call him a carpenter. We would call him a handyman. My husband is handy. My uncle is handy. My daddy is handy. You wouldn't call him a carpenter.

To be a carpenter, you have to be willing to build for other people. I'm a journeyman carpenter by trade, so I get that. So, what I'm doing as a carpenter is building for other people.

There are some people who have gotten wealthy, but they don't help others to generate wealth.

So, they are wealthy, and they have done something to get wealthy, but they do not have the ability to help others generate wealth. So, they are more a student of wealth than they are a teacher of wealth. And, what we have done as people is admire and follow the students of wealth as opposed to admiring and following the teachers of wealth.

For example, nobody here has ever been to a class about wealth from Jeff Bezos, yet we all know his name. As opposed to knowing the names of the people who helped him develop his wealth… you know the wrong names. You know the wrong people. You study and admire the wrong people. It's not the student that you're looking to learn from. It's the teacher. And so, I am a teacher of wealth. That's what I do. You are much more likely to hear the names of my students than you are to hear my name.

For example, let me tell you about one of my mentoring students, Holly from Maryland. When Holly came to me, she had a dead-end vending business that wasn't making her any money. Her mother was suffering from Alzheimer's, and she needed to be in a care home. I taught her how to invest in banknotes. I walked her through my course, and this is who she is now. Holly increased her net worth by $1.5 million dollars in 10 months. She made $400,000 on just one note deal.

Click the link below or scan the QR code to listen how Holly did that deal
https://www.youtube.com/watch?v=SyZYuc8RRpY

Another of my mentoring students, Ron, made $1.2 million dollars in one hour from buying a commercial note from a bank. Ron, a millionaire, came to me as an experienced investor who owned commercial buildings. He wanted to buy a property that was distressed from the bank, but the bank only wanted to sell the note and not the property. Ron didn't have any experience dealing directly with the bank until he called me to join my mentoring program.

Click the link below or scan QR code to view the video
Mentee Makes $1.2 Million Profit Buying A Commercial Note From A Bank
https://www.youtube.com/watch?v=TlhtmXCDiEM&t=19s

Wealth For The Rest Of Us is my movement. It's the song that I sing. A movement is a concept or idea that people rally together around.

When you're in the middle class or poor, you don't get a chance to have better schooling for your family. You don't get to have better housing. You don't get to have better healthcare. You don't get to have your dreams. If you are not born into a wealthy family, your kids go to jail. If you're born into a wealthy family, your kids go to Yale.

So, "Who are the rest of us"? The rest of us are the people who have dreams and aspirations and want a better life for ourselves and our families. We are the rest of us. We are the people who are trying to include ourselves in the wealth conversation.

The conversation around a better life. As opposed to excluding us from those types of conversations, we're looking for inclusion. And when we're talking about us, wealth is especially exclusionary and discriminatory when it comes to gender, race, the middle class, and the poor. If you fall into one of these categories, you're going to have a hard time generating wealth. Wealth is exclusionary, and it's discriminatory. So, I'm talking about how to build "WEALTH FOR THE REST OF US."

So, if any of you don't believe what I'm talking about, who pays more taxes, the wealthy or the poor? Everybody knows the answer… the poor… exactly!

If wealthy people make more money, then why do poor people pay more taxes? Now, here is the thing: you know that answer, and you know where it places you, but you don't know how to get out. Wealth has been an exclusionary proposition, and so for those of us caught in the middle, we call that the middle class. For those of us caught below the middle class, we call that the poor, right? All we're trying to figure out is how to escape this trap. We like to call it the wealth trap, and what happens is we're caught in this trap that feels like we can never get out.

So, we think the middle class is a way of success, but it's a prison that locks you out of your dreams. The middle class and poor are a type of prison. It's a prison with no physical walls, but it limits your life every day. You have to understand what wealth means for your life and what wealth means for your family and your bank account.

And if you want wealth for you and your family, I want you to now pay attention to what I'm going to be teaching you. I want you to take out your pen and start taking notes. Now you start to believe, and now you start to do.

Some of you have done more for other people's wealth than you've done for yourself because you believe in their wealth more than you believe in yours. You believe they have a right to your wealth. But when it comes to your own wealth, you believe that you have what you deserve.

Because you believe in somebody else's wealth more than you believe in your own wealth, you put more effort into their wealth than you did your own. That's why you did it.

And for many of you, you're afraid. So, today, you take out your pen. My name is Terry Bontemps, and I'm a teacher of wealth. I'm the No. 1 bank foreclosure mentor in the country. I'm here to mentor you on the path to generating real wealth. This is what this book is about. My book deals with any of your fears, your insecurities, and your doubts that you have about your credit or what's in your bank account.

Because for some of you, they've scared you away from wealth by saying, "Oh, what's your credit score?" And you immediately start to judge yourself. Some of you have been scared away from wealth because they asked you, "How much money do you have in your bank account?" Because there was a time when you couldn't even invest in certain stocks unless you had a certain income. You couldn't get a financial advisor unless you had a minimum of $100,000 in the bank. Minimum of six figures in the bank. If you didn't have $100,000 in your account, they wouldn't work with you.

Who is this book for? *WEALTH FOR THE REST OF US* is for you, if you're tired of feeling insecure because you feel like your credit score is a reflection of who you are not. I do not judge you based on your credit score. You can still generate wealth with a bad credit score or not.

WEALTH FOR THE REST OF US does not discriminate against people who have bad credit. It doesn't give greater credence to people who have an 800 credit score, or less to people who have a 500 credit score.

It's not about how much money, or how little you have in your bank account. *WEALTH FOR THE REST OF US* is about using the strategies that I'm going to teach you, and this is about taking action, consistent action in relationship to that.

So today, we're not talking about your wealth score. We're not talking about your credit score. We're not talking about how much money you have in your bank account. *WEALTH FOR THE REST OF US* is about your wealth habits. And right now, the biggest impediment to your wealth is not your credit score or how much you have in your bank account. The biggest impediment to your wealth is your habits.

Now, am I going to be dealing with all your habits? No. I am going to be dealing with your real estate habits. So today, I want you to write down the five millionaire habits that have made me wealthy, which will make you wealthy, too, because real estate is an equal opportunity wealth builder.

And wealth habit number one is acquiring property. Do you know what wealth habit number two is? Never forget rule number one.

RULE #1 — ACQUIRE PROPERTY

RULE #2 — DON'T FORGET RULE #1

These are the two wealth habits we're going to be working on. So, the only two questions you may have is:

#1 — How do you acquire property without having to necessarily leverage your credit score?

#2 — How do you acquire property without having to leverage your own money? But if you have plenty of money and good credit and you still want to leverage it, that's fine, too.

How do you do that? Keep reading, taking notes, and download my mobile app, Bank Foreclosure Millionaire, now!

MULTIPLY YOUR MONEY
REAL ESTATE
BE YOUR OWN BANK
DEBT FREE LIVING
BANK NOTE BUYING EXPERT
WEALTH BUILDING
ESTATE PLANNING
WEALTH
FOR THE REST OF US

Chapter 3 Takeaways and Actionable Steps
For You To Take

Chapter 3: Emphasizes the importance of real estate investing as a wealth-building strategy. The key takeaways from this chapter are:

1. **Real Estate Investing As A Wealth-Building Strategy**: Terry Bontemps emphasizes that real estate investing is one of the most effective ways to build wealth. He explains that real estate provides opportunities for cash flow, appreciation, tax benefits, and leverage.

2. **The Importance Of Mindset**: Bontemps emphasizes the importance of having the right mindset when it comes to wealth-building. He encourages readers to believe in their ability to acquire wealth and to overcome any limiting beliefs or negative thoughts they may have about money.

3. **The Wealth-Building Blueprint**: He provides a step-by-step blueprint for acquiring wealth through real estate investing. The blueprint includes the following steps:

   A) Set Clear Goals: Terry Bontemps advises readers to set clear and specific goals for their wealth-building journey. This includes setting financial targets, determining the desired lifestyle, and identifying the timeline for achieving these goals.

   B) Educate Yourself: Bontemps emphasizes the importance of acquiring knowledge and education about real estate investing. He encourages readers to read books, attend seminars, and seek out mentors who can provide guidance and support.

   C) Take Action: He emphasizes the importance of taking action and implementing what has been learned. He advises readers to start small and gradually build their real estate portfolio over time.

D) Build a Team: Terry Bontemps advises readers to build a team of professionals who can support their real estate investing journey. This includes finding a real estate agent, a mortgage broker, a property manager, and other professionals who can provide expertise and guidance.

E) Analyze Deals: Bontemps emphasizes the importance of analyzing real estate deals thoroughly. He provides guidance on how to evaluate properties, calculate potential profits, and assess risks.

F) Secure Financing: He advises readers to explore different financing options for their real estate investments. This includes traditional bank loans, private lenders, and partnerships.

G) Manage Properties: Terry Bontemps emphasizes the importance of effectively managing rental properties. He provides guidance on finding and screening tenants, handling maintenance and repairs, and maximizing rental income.

H) Monitor and Adjust: Bontemps advises readers to regularly monitor their real estate investments and make adjustments as needed. This includes reviewing financial performance, assessing market conditions, and making strategic decisions to optimize returns.

Actionable Items for Readers:

1. Set clear and specific goals for wealth-building through real estate investing.

2. Invest in education and acquire knowledge about real estate investing.

3. Take action and start small by investing in a first property.

4. Build a team of professionals who can support and guide the real estate investing journey.

5. Thoroughly analyze real estate deals before making investment decisions.

6. Explore different financing options and secure appropriate funding for investments.

7. Effectively manage rental properties by finding and screening tenants, handling maintenance, and maximizing rental income.

8. Regularly monitor real estate investments and make adjustments as needed to optimize returns.

Overall, Chapter 3 provides a comprehensive blueprint for acquiring wealth through real estate investing. It emphasizes the importance of mindset, education, action, and effective management in the wealth-building journey. The actionable items provided in the chapter can guide readers in taking practical steps towards achieving financial success through real estate investing.

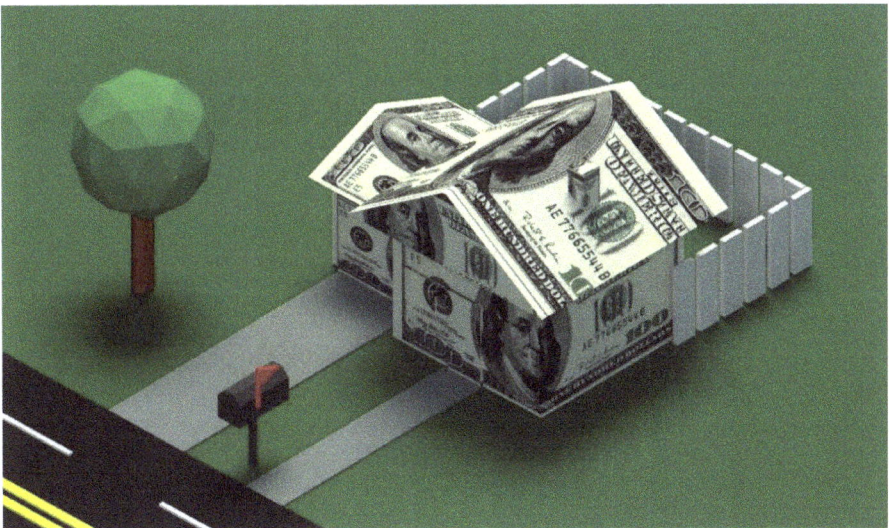

CHAPTER 4:
THE MOST POWERFUL
WEALTH-BUILDING
INVESTMENT
STRATEGY IN THE WORLD!

WEALTH HABIT #3:
BEING THE BANK

How did the banks become the richest, most powerful institutions in the world?

Take a look at your mortgage statement and the thousands of dollars in interest you've paid… that's why!

Put a stop to making the banks rich instead of you.

—Terry Bontemps

Learn how to make money, build wealth, and be a real estate millionaire. Teach your kids and teens about money, finance, and investing. Download Terry's mobile app Bank Foreclosure Millionaire from Amazon or Apple Store today, $19.99.

It's time for you to BE THE BANK. To start thinking like THE BANK, acting like THE BANK, and ultimately BECOMING THE BANK.

So, at the end of the day, you have to own the note. To be financially free, you have to own the note.

—Terry Bontemps

Acquiring property is the main way that people build wealth in this country. Without acquiring property, it's very difficult for you to build generational wealth and pass wealth down to your family. This is something that's not really understood by a lot of people. When you don't have money, it's hard to get by, but when you don't own any property, it's hard to get ahead.

The most powerful wealth-building strategy in the world is being the bank. So, it's time for you to learn how to BE YOUR OWN BANK so you can start acquiring property. To start thinking like the bank, acting like THE BANK and ultimately becoming THE BANK. So, at the end of the day, you've got to own the note, which ultimately controls property for you to make a profit from. To be financially free, you've got to own the note, the paper... the mortgage.

The thing about this is you're so happy about buying a home, and you should be. You're excited the bank is letting you buy a house. Of course, the banks are going to let you buy it, because the banks will get rich from you getting a mortgage. In essence, from the bank giving you a loan, you work for the bank once you sign the papers.

You now have a commitment to basically get a job so you can continue to make the payments on that note... to the person who really owns the property, which is the bank.

You know how we walk around saying, "I work for the government?" No, you work for the bank that owns your note. You really work for Wells Fargo, Bank of America, or Chase because they've got the note that secures the loan to your home. You go to your job every day for the next 30+ years, so you can pay the note on your house, your credit cards, your student loans, and the blue Jaguar in your driveway that are controlled by the bank.

EVERYBODY ELSE WILL BE TELLING YOU HOW TO BE A WHOLESALER, A LANDLORD, AND A FIX AND FLIPPER TO MAKE A PROFIT BUYING AND SELLING HOUSES

Did you see what happened to Redfin, Opendoor, and Zillow? They went out there buying, fixing, and trying to flip houses. It almost took their companies out. They had the money, and they had lots of it. They had plenty of money; they had it in droves, but you know what? They didn't speak the language of the bank. They didn't think about being the bank. Redfin, Opendoor, and Zillow didn't think, act, or invest like the bank. They invested like customers and house flippers… and in the end, that was their demise.

We spend too much time watching *Flip This House* on television. We imagine ourselves being landlords, wholesalers and fix and flippers. But if you're trying to get wealthy, you have to think, act and invest like the banks. Banks think own the note… buy the note, be the bank, and get rich!

Real estate people think buy it and flip it. Bank people think, own the note… buy the note, be the bank, get rich! One can put you in the poorhouse, and the other can make you wealthy!

Why don't we talk more about notes? Because you can't go put a marble countertop on a note. Notes are not sexy and they're not pretty, but they will make you wealthy.

BANKS TRY TO OWN YOUR COMPLETE DESTINY WITH A NOTE – A PIECE OF PAPER

Banks are continuously creating greater ways to keep you in debt by giving you notes attached to property and things you think you own. Banks try to own your complete financial destiny with a piece of paper.

And most people avoid the paper, never realizing that the paper is what banks have used to enslave them financially year, after year, after year!

A note is the process by which the bank will sell you something for two to three times or more than it's worth. I teach people how to own the note. Everybody who wants to stay in debt, keep doing what you've been doing. I set people free through the power of real estate notes.

The number one reason why you have to learn about notes is because you need to know about the systems banks have used to financially enslave you, your family, and your money, so that it won't ever happen again

ALL BANKS KEEP DOING IS CREATING NEW WAYS TO OWN AND CONTROL PEOPLE FINANCIALLY

Banks own you financially through your car note. They own you financially through your house note, second mortgages, equity loans, "buy now- pay later" loans, and 401k loans. They own you financially through your student loans, business loans, credit cards, and payday loans.

Your whole life is secured by a note, a piece of paper… then it's like the banks are aiming for your kids, too. They want them to go to college, which means they will need student loans. They want a note on your kids so that they control them financially, too. Banks keep creating new ways by which they own people financially. And the reason why banks are able to do it is because of your lack of knowledge about notes.

The banks are offering you loans for every single financial decision that you make in life to solve your lack of money problems, and they're bankrupting you. Banks keep creating greater ways to keep you in debt by giving you notes attached to property and things you think you own. There are higher things to aspire towards than being a doctor or a lawyer. In most households, we're told that when we grow up, we need to be a doctor or lawyer. Don't tell your kids to become doctors or lawyers. Instead, tell them to be bankers. Because guess what? All of them doctors and lawyers got notes owned by the banks.

We call them student loans. Banks just keep creating new ways to own and control people financially. And the more you keep participating in the process of basically allowing your life to be secured by a note, the deeper in debt you will be. A bank can own you financially without you even knowing it. Banks dictate behavior.

Everything begins and ends with the bank, and that's the only thing you can become in this world that gives you ultimate freedom and power. Since the beginning of time, everybody has answered to the bank. I'm not trying to teach you how to be an investor or customer. I'm teaching you how to BE THE BANK!

BECOME YOUR OWN BANK

Step #1 to becoming the bank is learning how to speak the language of the bank. Those other gurus, coaching and training programs in the real estate education space are speaking the language of the seller... talk to the seller who owns the property that's making mortgage payments to the bank (who owns the note). The buyer or investor must talk to the seller to buy their property so they can live in it to profit from it.

THE LANGUAGE OF BANKS

They're speaking the language of the seller. And so, they're constantly going to find sellers of real estate – this seller, and that seller, because they're speaking the language of the seller, whose house is actually owned by the bank, right?

Step #2 is becoming the bank, and Step #3 is becoming bankable. I'm teaching you how to speak the language of the banks:

#1 – Make an offer to the bank, not the property owner, to make a profit.

#2 – Neither the owner of the property nor the real estate agent is involved in this process, so neither of them has to be notified or know when you're buying directly from the bank.

The biggest problem that most of these real estate courses and gurus have is that most of them are still speaking a language that will never actually help you to become wealthy.

Why? Because they're teaching you how to speak the wrong language. You're speaking the language of the buyer and seller. And not that the buyer and seller are not important, but... You have to understand that, in the order of priority, the bank is always at the top. The bank always gets paid when the property is sold or refinanced, and they always get paid first. The seller of the property gets paid after the bank.

So, at the end of the day... I'll give you a perfect example. Rarely are you going to see the president of the United States go and meet with the vice president of another country.

Presidents want to talk to presidents, right?

And so, what starts to happen is you are talking to the vice president, but you want to be talking to the president. And the problem is that real estate investors don't really get that for the most part. It's buying, renting, and flipping. But you can profit from real estate in a bigger and better way on a much larger level. The bank has no liability, management, repairs, or fix and flipping costs involved, nor do they pay real estate commissions, closing costs, etc.

Sellers, buyers, and investors are constantly thinking about buying one property and flipping one property at a time... when, instead, they could've bought several bank notes or a portfolio of loans at one time.

PROFITING FROM REAL ESTATE IN A BIGGER AND BETTER WAY ON A MUCH LARGER LEVEL

Investors are thinking about buying one property at a time. As a banknote buyer, I'm thinking about getting wealthy by buying a bundle or package of properties at one time. At the same time.

1. It's not based on your credit, and

2. It's not based on how much money you have in your bank account.

It's based upon you speaking the language of the bank. So, if powerful people ask powerful questions, here is the question. Do you speak the language of the banks? Let me give you an example. When I went to Hawaii, I did not speak the language of the land, and because I didn't speak the language, I ended up paying extra for everything.

I was unfamiliar with the culture and the cost of things within that culture. Well, if you're unfamiliar with the culture of the bank and the way banks value its assets, it means you don't speak their language, so you're going to overpay for everything.

YOU EITHER SPEAK THE LANGUAGE OF THE BANKS, OR YOU SPEAK THE LANGUAGE OF THE CUSTOMER. WHICH LANGUAGE DO YOU SPEAK?

So, if the bank can get you to pay two, three, four, or more times what their real estate is worth, they're going to do that. But the only reason you end up in a situation like that is because you don't speak the language of the bank.

Let me give you an example. When you speak the language of a customer, you speak customer rather than speaking the language of the bank. Because there are two types of languages, you speak either customer or bank, right?

If you speak customer, right, the customer says, "This is how much money I have, and here's my credit score. What can I buy?"

And the bank says, "Well, you don't have enough money, but we will give you a mortgage. We're going to give you some interest with that mortgage, and you're going to pay our bank two to three times or more than what the property's worth if you want to buy a home for you and your family."

CUSTOMERS ONLY KNOW TWO THINGS:
#1 – MONEY IN THEIR ACCOUNT, #2 –THEIR CREDIT SCORE

Banks are never really trying to use their money to acquire and control property. Even with some of the biggest deals that you've seen in the world, it's been a swap of stock. They are not using their money to acquire properties. They're only using it in situations where it's an absolute necessity. But as a customer, you use what's in your bank account and your credit score as the first and only option to acquire real estate.

Customers only know two things. #1 – money in their account, and #2 – their credit score. If you speak bank, that's how Donald Trump can file for bankruptcy and still be one of the richest people in the world. Why? Because he knows it's not based upon credit, and he knows that it's not based on how much money he has in his bank account. Donald Trump speaks bank.

I'm going to teach you how to speak bank, and how to understand what the banks value so you can properly position your offer so that you can acquire bank foreclosures for pennies on the dollar, without even leveraging your credit and capital. That's what it's all about. Do you speak bank? And the answer for most sellers, buyers, and investors is they don't.

And the moment that you open your mouth... Just like, for example, I'm American. If you open your mouth, even if you speak American but are not really from America, I can hear your accent. It's rough. So, you've got to learn to speak bank, and you got to speak bank fluently. Then, after you start doing that, you start making deals, and you become the bank.

A MORTGAGE IS A PROCESS BY WHICH THE BANK SELLS YOU A HOUSE FOR 2 TO 3 TIMES OR MORE THAN IT'S WORTH

Now, you become the person who is making the deals. So, this is what being bankable means. The bank is looking to basically sell its assets to customers who will pay more than what a property is worth. This is why they're giving people mortgages, which is the process by which you are buying a house for more than it's worth.

The bank gives you a mortgage for $150,000, but by the time you pay it off, you've paid back $300,000 to 350,000 or more to the bank.

Who wouldn't like to sell a $150,000 property for two to three times or more than what it's worth? Wouldn't you?

That's what a mortgage is. It's the process by which a bank can sell a customer a property or a real estate asset for two to three times or more than what it's worth. That is the purpose of the bank giving you a mortgage.

So, in customer language, the purpose of a mortgage is to have a home to raise your family in and live the American dream. In bank language, it is the process of selling a property for two to three times or more than its worth.

So, do you speak customer, or do you speak bank?

It's time for you to BECOME THE BANK. Now is the time for you to start selling properties for two to three times or more than what you paid for them. Now, you start building a wealth portfolio and become the banker. When you do this, you become the type of person that banks are eager to do business with.

BANKS HOLD THE PAPER AND CONTROL THE FINANCING ON REAL ESTATE IN EVERY NEIGHBORHOOD IN THE WORLD

In every city and state that you go to on the planet Earth, there's always a banking system in place. Everybody knows the names of the banks in those areas. You think about the biggest names in every city: Bank of America, Wells Fargo, Chase... right?

The banks have the greatest degree of power in any city or state that you go to. Go to Mexico, they have Mexican banks, they know the name of the bank. You go to Jamaica, and they have Jamaican banks.

The banks hold the paper and control the financing on properties in every neighborhood in the world, which makes them the richest and most powerful institutions on the planet.

If you want to be a powerful person, you've got to become bankable. The only way you become bankable is to start buying bank notes to control the financing and the property.... **BE THE BANK!**

My unique seller proposition is that I'm going to teach you how to speak bank. Everybody else will be telling you about how to be a landlord. Everybody else will be telling you how to be a wholesaler, how to fix it and flip it.

Did you see what happened to Redfin, Opendoor, and Zillow? They started buying houses above market value, they had the money, and they had lots of it. They had plenty of money, and they had it in droves, but you know what? They didn't speak bank. You want to know what else? They didn't think about **BEING THE BANK**.

So, they went out there buying property, fixing them, and trying to flip houses. It almost took their company out. Zillow almost had to file for bankruptcy. The CEO of Zillow came out and said, "Look, we're not buying any more properties." Opendoor lost $1 billion in Q3.

ZILLOW, OPENDOOR, AND REDFIN ALL TRIED TALKING THE LANGUAGE OF A CUSTOMER, SPENT MILLIONS, AND THEY GOT IT WRONG

Now, think about it. These companies had hundreds of millions of dollars, and they couldn't necessarily master the house-buying and flipping process. They all got it wrong.

You want to know why? Because they were thinking like the customer, saying, "Let's go buy this property from a seller and see how much we can flip it for." They were thinking buy and flip, versus own the note… buy the note, be the bank, and get rich.

WHEN MOST PEOPLE THINK ABOUT REAL ESTATE, THEY THINK ABOUT THE PHYSICAL PROPERTY AND NOT THE NOTE (THE PAPER)

Real estate people think buy it and flip it. Bank people think, own the note… buy the note, be the bank, and get rich. If you own the note, you control the property and profits without owning the property. When you own the note, you don't deal with all the headaches of maintenance, management, and liability. But see, you can own the property and not own the note.

Your mother, father, brother, and uncle own property. They don't own the note on that property.

There are different levels to this real estate game. Because if you truly own the property, you own the note.

When you get a mortgage, you just get to feel like you own the property. You get to live on the property. You get to raise your family on the property, but you don't own the property.

So, basic-level real estate people think… buy it, fix it, and flip it. But banks think, own the note, buy the note, be the bank, and get rich. Do you own the note, or are you buying properties and selling properties?

One can put you in a poor house, and the other can make you wealthy. The most powerful wealth-building strategy in the world is being the bank, and owning bank notes. We spend too much time watching *Flip That House* on television, and we imagine ourselves being real estate gurus, landlords, wholesalers, and fix and flippers. Investors are knocking on doors and grabbing lock boxes. If you like designing houses, then that's ok, and more power to you, but if you're really trying to get wealthy, you have to think like the banks. They think, own the note… buy the note, be the bank, get rich!

And you want to know something funny? Even when it comes to buying cars… banks don't want to own the car, they want to own the note. Banks want to own the paper, the financing, the note.

BANKS THINK OWN THE NOTE… BUY THE NOTE, BE THE BANK, GET RICH!

It's funny because when you first buy a car, they say you got a car note. There are only two words: car note, or free and clear. You have a car note. The bank owns the note. They let you drive their car, and you pay the note. And then, when you finally own it, they give it to you free and clear.

And then you sell it to somebody else so that you can buy another car, but you're not really buying it, right? You're getting another note.

But it all comes down to the paper. Banks think, own the note… buy the note, be the bank, get rich! They're not selling cars, they're selling notes. The bank gets dealerships to sell the cars attached to the note they own.

Banks don't own dealerships. They own paper, the notes, financing. Banks don't own dealerships. Dealerships bring the person who wants to buy a car to the banks. They say, "We have a person. Here's their credit, and here's how much money they have. Can you give them a note so they can buy a car?"

The note is the process by which the bank will sell you something for two to three times or more than its worth. You bought a car for $20,000, but by the time you pay it off, you pay $35,000, or more.

It's really simple: I teach people how to own the note. I'm not begging anybody to be free, right? Everybody who wants to stay in debt, keep doing what you've been doing. I am looking to set people free financially through the power of real estate notes. Let's be clear: I help people like yourself buy and own notes so that you can become the bank and build generational wealth.

"Those who understand interest are destined to earn it, while those that don't are doomed to pay it."

ALL BANKS KEEP DOING IS CREATING NEW WAYS TO OWN AND CONTROL YOU, YOUR FAMILY, AND YOUR MONEY

And the more you keep participating in the process of basically allowing your life to be secured by a note, the deeper in debt you will be.

It's the reason why you will work for the rest of your life, and never be financially free unless you start thinking and doing differently right now.

—Terry Bontemps

Chapter 4 Takeaways and Actionable Steps
For You To Take

Chapter 4: Discusses the wealth-building investment strategy of being the bank. Here are the key takeaways and actionable items from this chapter:

1. **Importance Of Being The Bank**: The chapter emphasizes the power and profitability of being the bank in real estate investing. It highlights how banks have become the richest institutions in the world by utilizing this very profitable investing strategy.

2. **Buying Notes And Mortgages:** The chapter explains how investors can buy notes and mortgages from banks, which allows them to become the lender and collect interest payments from borrowers. This strategy provides a consistent cash flow and the potential for high double even triple or higher interest rate returns.

3. **Benefits Of Note Buying**: The chapter outlines the benefits of note buying, including the ability to generate passive income, build wealth, and create generational wealth. It also mentions that note buying does not require good credit or a large amount of capital.

4. **Steps To Becoming The Bank**: The chapter provides a step-by-step process for becoming the bank in real estate investing. This includes finding deals, evaluating the financials, negotiating with banks, and managing the investment.

5. **Key Performance Indicators (KPIs):** The chapter emphasizes the importance of using KPIs to evaluate real estate deals. It mentions KPIs such as total profit, return on investment, profit margin percentage, equity, and buying real estate on the dollar. These KPIs help investors assess the profitability and risk of a deal.

6. **Multiplying And Increasing Investment**: The chapter

discusses the concept of multiplying and increasing investment in real estate. It explains how investors can make significant profits by buying properties for pennies on the dollar and leveraging their investments.

7. **Actionable Items**: The actionable items for the reader include:

   A) Educate oneself about note buying and the process of becoming the bank.

   B) Learn about the key performance indicators and how to use them to evaluate real estate deals.

   C) Research and identify potential opportunities to buy notes or mortgages from banks.

   D) Develop a disciplined investment process and framework for evaluating real estate deals.

   E) Consider partnering with experienced investors or mentors who can provide guidance and support in note buying.

Overall, the chapter highlights the immense potential of being the bank in real estate investing and provides actionable steps for readers to start implementing this strategy.

CHAPTER 5:
NOTES ARE HOW BANKS CONTROL REAL ESTATE AND THE FINANCING, WHICH IS HOW THEY'VE BECOME THE RICHEST AND MOST POWERFUL INSTITUTIONS IN THE WORLD

THE MONEY-MAKING STRATEGY THAT BANKS AND THE FINANCIAL POWERS THAT BE NEVER WANTED YOU TO KNOW

The wealthiest real estate investing strategy in the world is owning notes! The bank lends $300,000. It will make back the $300,000 and $400,489 of profit if the owner makes every payment. That's a 133% return on investment for the bank. The bank is MULTIPLYING its money 2.5 TIMES, and they have no maintenance, management, or liability!

—Terry Bontemps

How did banks become the richest institutions in the world?

By owning notes…

Terry, why don't we talk more about notes? Notes are not sexy; they're not pretty, but that's the financial vehicle that makes banks wealthy. It's how banks make money… LOTS OF IT!

Albert Einstein said something that I want you guys to remember and write it down. He said, "Those that understand interest are destined to earn it while those that don't are doomed to pay it."

First of all, the largest buildings in my neighborhood are controlled by the banks. The banks control the largest buildings because they own the notes.

See, the money is in the financing, the debt against the property, which is the note. How did banks become the richest, most powerful institutions in the world?

It's simple take a look at your mortgage statement for those of you who are buying a house.

It's all the interest payments that the bank receives. When you start looking at the profits (the interest) that the banks make, I think I'm going to get on the side of the bankers myself. So, let's put a stop to the banks getting rich instead of us.

I want you guys to say this, "Terry, show me the money!" For us note buyers, it's in the truth and lending disclosure statement. Below is a note. This is what I look for as a note buyer. Some of you who are in the residential market are more concerned with the houses. I want the note, the paper. So, if you take a real close look at this, someone went out and financed $300,000 to buy a house, and they financed it at 6.75%.

Over the life of this loan, if the borrower made every payment for the full 30 years, the bank is going to make $400,000 in interest, which is their profit. The borrower will pay back a total of $700,489 for borrowing $300,000.

IS THIS CRAZY? IT'S $400,000 OF INTEREST THAT THE BORROWER WILL PAY BACK TO THE BANK? Yes, it is crazy if you're paying it, but if you're on the receiving side like the bank, which I like to be, this is wonderful. I'd like to have that $400,000 of interest/ profit deposited in my bank account. I'm excited about it. You do this by owning the note. I will try and buy this note from the bank at a discount.

People buy houses like this every day, all day, 365 days a year. I've bought houses using banks also. It's what you do if you want to buy a house and you can't pay all cash.

Over 88% Of Your First Payment Goes To Interest...
Does This Sound Like 7%?

Payment#	Balance	Payment	Interest	Principal	New Balance
1	$300,000	$1,996	$1,750	$246	$299,754
60	$282,741	$1,996	$1,649	$347	$282,395
120	$257,928	$1,996	$1,505	$491	$257,437
240	$172,888	$1,996	$1,009	$987	$143,250
359	$3,957	$1,996	$23	$1,973	$1,984

Take a look at this. On the first payment on that $300,000 loan, the monthly payment is $1,996.

$1,750 goes to interest, and only $246 goes to the principal. A total of 88% of the first payment goes to interest. That doesn't sound like 6.75% to me. Sounds a lot higher. Think about it. Look down to where it says 240th payment. If you go all the way to the right, it's going to take you 240 payments before you'll have half of the balance paid off.

After 20 years, the borrower has paid over $336,000 in interest, which we'll call the bank's profit. That's interesting. We need to start acting more like bankers instead of being on the other side of owning the property.

Click the link below or scan the QR code to watch video
How Banks Became The Richest Institutions in the World
https://www.youtube.com/watch?v=3f2TRifS1Nk

WHAT IS A NOTE?

Now, let's talk about the note. The bank has three pieces of information. They have the note that I showed you earlier. They have the house as collateral, and the deed of trust or mortgage, depending on what state you're doing business in.

WHY BUY NOTES?

The reason we buy notes is because we want to control the real estate transaction. If we do that, we control the house. You guys have all heard that the rich control, but they don't own. I've never seen this in real life, except for notes. Again, you don't own the property – you own the note, okay?

NOTE BUYING WORKS ON ANY LOAN SECURED BY REAL ESTATE

Note buying works on any loan that's secured by real estate that's in default. So, a non- performing note is from a property in which someone has not made payments. These are the ones I like. They create a lot of opportunities for someone like me who buys notes. You can buy the notes on multi-family, luxury homes, apartments, office buildings, self-storage, marinas, and mobile home parks.

HOW TO MAKE MONEY BUYING NOTES

There are seven different profitable exit strategies or seven different ways you can get paid for owning notes. Foreclosure, refinance, sell, the deed-in-lieu of foreclosure, the short sale, cash for keys, and a loan modification.

I'm just brushing through this quickly, and I'll go into more detail later. I love the exit strategies because they are the different ways in which you can make money. Now, if you're a house buyer, there are only two ways that you make money. You can buy and sell, and/or you can buy and hold.

NOTE BUYING HAS NOTHING TO DO WITH BEING A LANDLORD

I am a landlord, but this note business has nothing to do with being a landlord. For one of the properties that I still own, the people moved in and they were great for eight years. What happened was that they got involved with crank and meth. They had pit bull dogs on the inside and the outside, and I could not go into my own house. It was crazy! The city of fined me $500 for the property being a public nuisance. Guess what? I went in, cleaned it up, got it looking a lot nicer and rented it back out again. So, again, this note business has nothing to do with being a landlord. Okay? There's no maintenance. You never have to paint, do repairs, and fix toilets. Think about it. If you own your house right now, does the bank ever come out and do any repairs? No, they don't, and I like that!

You never have to pay retail for houses again. There's no liability, and there are no management responsibilities. If someone falls down on the property and decides to sue, who are they going to sue? They normally sue the owner. They don't sue the bank, which is another advantage to being the bank. Again, I've been doing this since 2001, and when I first started, I couldn't believe the money I was making. I thought something was wrong because I couldn't find anybody else who was doing the same thing. I decided just keep doing it. Now, all of a sudden, it's a really hot market. Again, there are no liability or management responsibilities.

There is never any need to ask the permission of the homeowner. You don't need permission from the homeowner to buy the note. I can buy houses and control houses without the owner's permission.

WHEN YOU OWN THE NOTE, YOU DON'T OWN THE PROPERTY

When you buy the note, you don't own the property, okay? You own the note and the mortgage, not the property.

THERE'S TWO WAYS TO LOSE YOUR MONEY WHEN BUYING NOTES

There are two ways you can lose when you invest and buy notes. Write this down. IF YOU PAY TOO MUCH FOR THE NOTE, and YOU DON'T KNOW WHAT YOU'RE DOING. These are the two ways you lose in the note-buying business.

Click the link below or scan the QR code to watch the video
What is Note Buying
https://www.youtube.com/watch?v=juupqvMk0OU

Listening to the traditional criteria for building wealth is keeping you poor. You were told that you need credit, experience, and capital by bankers, realtors, and the real estate industry to buy a home, invest in real estate, and build generational wealth. These myths are simply NOT TRUE! I'm going to show you how to do it.

So many deserving people, including minorities, marginalized communities, and the working class have been locked out of the wealth-building experience due to simply believing the myths and conventional thinking of bankers and realtors.

Wealth has eluded you not because of money, credit and experience but because you're missing the savvy, the strategy, the mentorship, the consistency, and the know-how.

Real estate is an equal opportunity wealth builder. One of the biggest problems with wealth in this country is the lack of inclusion of the middle class, and the poor.

I'm making wealth accessible, equitable, and inclusive for anyone with zero barriers, regardless of your credit score, previous investing experience, or what you have in your bank account...

—Terry Bontemps

Chapter 5 Takeaways and Actionable Steps
For You To Take

Chapter 5: Discusses the importance of notes in real estate and how banks use them to control real estate and financing. Here are the key takeaways from this chapter:

1. Notes are the paper or mortgage that represents the debt owed on a property. Banks hold these notes as assets and use them to generate income through interest payments.

2. Banks have become the richest and most powerful institutions in the world because they control the financing of real estate. By lending money to borrowers and holding the notes, banks have the power to dictate the terms of the loan and ultimately control the property.

3. Investing in notes can be a lucrative strategy for building wealth in real estate. By purchasing notes from banks at a discounted price, investors can earn passive income through interest payments and potentially acquire the property if the borrower defaults.

4. The key to success in note investing is understanding the numbers and analyzing the potential profitability of the investment. This includes evaluating the total profit, return on investment, time to get investment back, profit margin percentage, equity, buying real estate on the dollar, and multiplied and increased investment.

5. The chapter emphasizes the importance of financial education and understanding key performance indicators (KPIs) in real estate investing. By knowing the numbers and analyzing the data, investors can make informed decisions and increase their chances of success.

Actionable items for the reader:

- Educate yourself on the concept of notes and how they work in real estate.

- Learn about key performance indicators (KPIs) and how to analyze them to evaluate potential investments.
- Consider investing in notes as a strategy for building wealth in real estate.
- Seek out resources and mentors who can provide guidance and support in note investing.
- Develop a disciplined investment process and a proven framework for evaluating real estate deals.
- Continuously educate yourself on financial matters and stay updated on industry trends and strategies.

CHAPTER 6:
AS AN INVESTOR,
YOUR JOB IS TO MULTIPLY YOUR MONEY,
INCREASE YOUR CASH FLOW,
AND BUILD GENERATIONAL WEALTH

WEALTH HABIT #4: MULTIPLYING YOUR MONEY

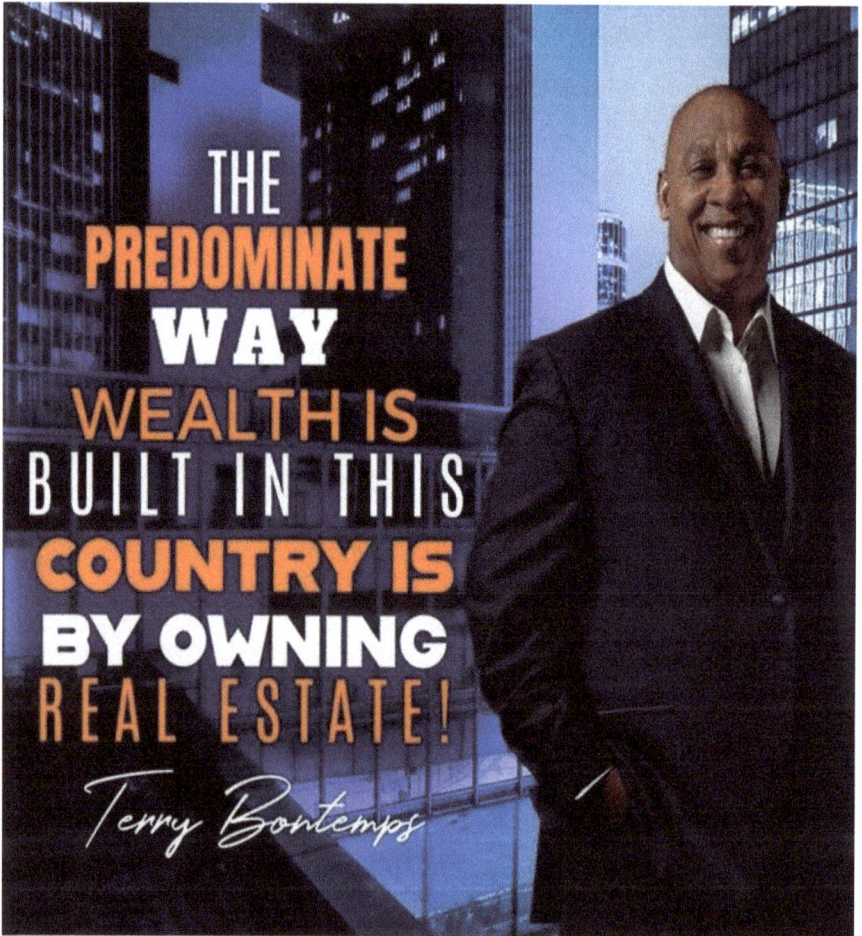

THE **PREDOMINATE** WAY WEALTH IS BUILT IN THIS COUNTRY IS BY OWNING REAL ESTATE!

Terry Bontemps

***What would you do with your life if you didn't
have to go to a job every single day because you
didn't need to work for money anymore?***

Ladies and gentlemen, I want you to understand what I'm about to do. Follow me… in order for you to have and build wealth, you must know how wealth is built.

The predominant way wealth is built in this country is by owning real estate – 90% of this country's millionaires created their wealth in real estate. You have to learn and know how wealth is built by owning real estate.

If you don't know anything about what I'm getting ready to teach you right now, you'll have a hard time building wealth. I'm going to teach you how I invest my money and multiply it by making a 54% return on my investment.

You may ask, "Terry, what does 54% return on investment mean, and why is that important?" It simply means that for every dollar I invest, I will get a return of 54 cents. If you didn't know how to do this with your money, you could never do it.

So, again, you have to know how wealth is built in order for you to have and build wealth. A lot of us have seen people go to the job and get a paycheck. People who have wealth built their wealth by owning income-producing properties, businesses, and real estate.

What have you done financially in your life? Have you built wealth, or have you done what everybody else has done by going to a job and working for a paycheck? I'm showing you how to build generational wealth by owning real estate.

You must learn how to invest, multiply your money, and build wealth by owning real estate or else you're going to keep working for money, living paycheck-to-paycheck, saying, "I don't have any money."

You don't have any money because you didn't learn how to have your money work for you. You didn't learn how to invest, make money, and build wealth while you sleep.

I'm trying to get you a new money mindset to think about regarding working for a paycheck versus building wealth. The rich don't have jobs. You guys know that the rich don't work for money. They make money work for them! I'm sure you have heard that, but no one has shown you how that's done in real life. I'm doing it right now.

I'm showing you how it's done.

Understand this, you guys: when I invest my money, I know what return I want on my investment and how long it will take me to get my money back, because I've learned how to have my money work for me instead of me working hard for money.

I've learned how my money can make more money, instead of me working by the hour for a paycheck.

I bought a note from a bank for $10,000. I got a 54% return from that $10,000 investment. If I could get that owner to make their $454.42 monthly payment, I would get my $10,000 investment back in 22 months. For every dollar I invested in this deal, I would make 54 cents in return.

You ask, "Terry, I don't have any money to invest in real estate because I'm living paycheck-to-paycheck. I don't have any money to invest in real estate."

When will you get the money? There's a reason you don't have the money. It's because you haven't learned how to invest, so your money can work hard for you.

You don't know how to have your money working hard for you at night while you sleep.

You're used to getting up, going to the job, punching a clock, getting a check, and then that check is gone. That's living paycheck to paycheck!

I'm not talking down to you, but you're working hard for the money. You've got to learn how to make your money work hard for you. I put $10,000 into a real estate investment to get $454.42 a month.

Every first of the month, I get a check for $454.42 because I own real estate. I don't work for that money. That money comes to me month, after month, after month.

And then I get my investment of $10,000 back, and that money just keeps on working and working. It's called passive income, which means it comes whether I do anything or not. To get that $454.42, all I have to do is keep breathing.

You may say, "But Terry, you don't understand. I don't have any money to invest in real estate. You just don't understand."

You don't need money… you need the know-how. People think that money makes the real estate deal. Money doesn't make the deal.

You guys, if you don't have money, that qualifies you because if you can't make money without money, you aren't going to be able to make money with money.

It's your thinking… your education… your knowledge… your experience… your intellectual capital… that's what makes you money when you invest. The money is just a tool. So, you sit around and say, "Terry, I don't have any money. I have no money!"

Maybe if you learned how to invest in real estate so that you don't need to use your own money and your own credit, then maybe you could make some money. Then maybe you'll have some money to pay off your debts.

You would have some extra money to pay cash for what you want. One day, you can quit your job, like I did. I told my boss he was fired. I fired him before he could fire me. I told him I was losing money coming into the job, because I knew how to make money in real estate. I said, "If I spent my time working on real estate instead of being at this job, I'd have more money."

I'd have more free time. I could spend more quality time with my family and friends. I could spend time with my kids, and go to their school activities. I could volunteer at my church because I have free time. There's no true freedom like financial freedom! I'm financially free because I own real estate.

I could spend quality time in my community, making it better. I can take care of my mother and father, who are getting older. I can own a home and put my family in that home, take care of them, and love them because I own this home.

You can buy another home for the elderly, for women, for kids. Make them your mission in life so you can make an impact, change the world and be a role model in their lives.

I've got two students. Miss B and Ms. Lloyd. They're in Georgia. They want to open up a home for women who are having challenges. They want to open their home to take care of women. They want to treat them well, feed them, spend quality time with them, take care of them and love them. I said, "Come on, you guys, real estate can pay for that dream. LET'S GO!"

What is your mission in life? If you didn't have a job and you didn't have to worry about finances, what would you do in life with all the free time you have because you no longer have to work for money anymore?

What would you do with your life if you didn't have to go to a job every single day because you didn't need to work for money?

Working at a job doing something you don't love makes you tired. You're tired of going to work every day, day after day.

When you get home from working 8 to 10 hours a day, you're tired. You may have to go in on the weekends, you're tired, you're in the struggle – no money, but you have to keep going to work to pay the bills.

I haven't had a job in forever… as a matter of fact, since 1992. I wish you could see the smile on my face. The reason why is because I'm financially free. There's no true freedom like financial freedom!

I'm telling you, you don't need money. Money helps if you have it. I had the $10,000 for the deal that I wanted to invest in. Let me tell you guys, you need the knowledge on how to do what I'm doing.

When you know this, you can find people who have money and show them how you can give them a great return on their investment.

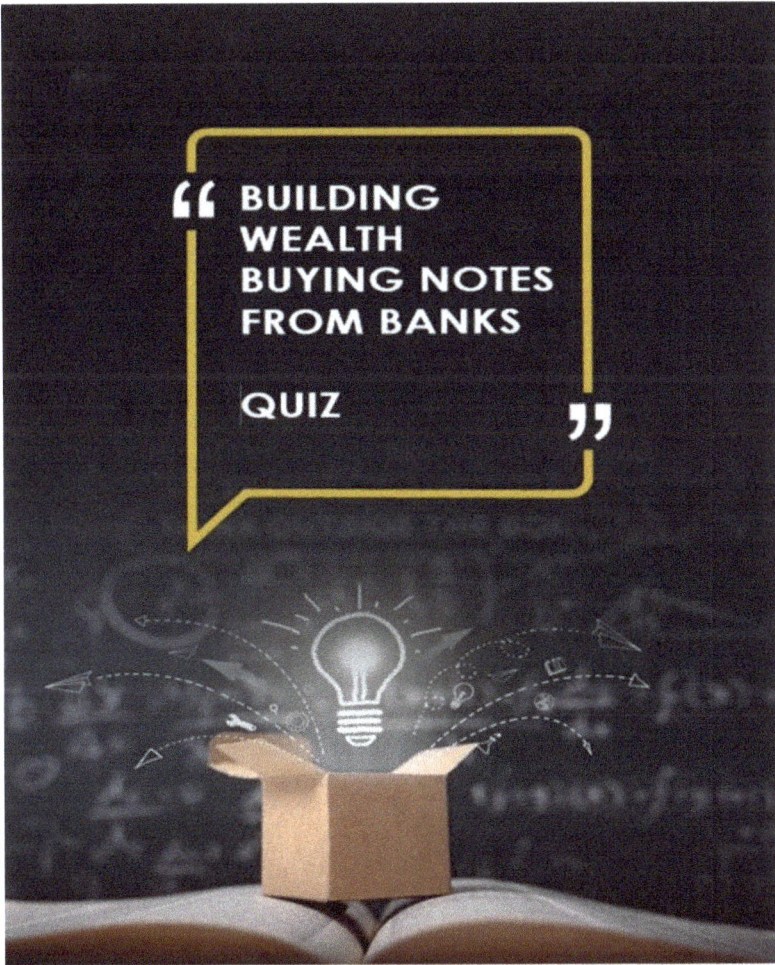

BUILDING WEALTH BUYING NOTES FROM BANKS

QUIZ

Led by Terry Bontemps, this workshop provides insight into making money from notes in real estate and identifies how to start with nothing but a calculator.

The most powerful real estate investment strategy in the world is buying notes. This is how banks get rich. Today, I am going to teach you and show you how to make money investing in real estate notes. I will teach you how to be an investor who makes money buying notes like I do by just starting with nothing but your calculator.

When it comes to notes, buying real estate and building wealth, you need to know your KPIs, which stands for Key Performance Indicators. The KPIs are the data you need to determine whether a deal is worthy of investing in. When you invest your money, one of the key performance indicators you need to know is how long it's going to take to get your money back. That's a key statistic and a key indicator that determines if you should do the deal or not.

For most people, when it comes to looking at the data and analyzing it, what do they do? They guess.

They have no way of analyzing the deal. They're using no logic. They're just using emotion. And then they wonder why they lose their money. They're basing their investment decisions on feelings, and that's a sure way to lose your money.

As an investor, your job is to multiply, increase, and grow your money. That's what an investor does. Today is all about how to buy notes from banks that multiply your money and build wealth without using your own cash or credit.

BUILDING WEALTH BY BEING THE BANK THROUGH BUYING NOTES

I'm going to show you guys how to find a partner, a money partner, and you're going to split your deals with that money partner 50/50. You've got the knowledge. You've got the smarts. You've got the know-how to find great real estate deals. Your money partner is going to put up the money, and you're going to split 50/50. Look, you do need money. Money helps. But you also need knowledge. It doesn't have to be your money. It can be someone else's money that funds the deal.

HOW TO FIND POTENTIAL REAL ESTATE DEALS

People who are not able to make their mortgage payments are who I work with. There are so many reasons why people can't make their mortgage payments. These people are who you should be trying to reach to see if they've got some real estate that they want to sell, keep, or give away. And if they're in foreclosure, they may have a note that you can buy from the bank to produce the type of results that you seek.

There are homeowners who cannot make their mortgage payments. They're on a forbearance plan because their job has been furloughed. Their job is never coming back. They don't have the money to make the mortgage payment. A family member may inherit real estate, and the family member just wants to get rid of it quickly. They will sell it at a discount.

There are people who are divorcing from too much time together. They have a property. They have a house. They decide to split up. That is your customer.

Why? Because you may have a solution to help them solve this problem. Because if they don't solve it, they don't get it taken care of. You have solutions. You have answers. This is your client. If their home is in foreclosure, you can try buying their note from the bank.

Death, debt, divorce, and distress will allow you to buy at a discount so that you can make some dollars. There also are people who are just giving their houses away. You just have to know how to ask, and they will give them to you.

Let's look at an example of a property in which you could buy a note. A couple took out a second mortgage on their home. They borrowed $35,000 for 20 years. The interest rate is 14.75% over 240 months.

The monthly payment is $454.42. Ultimately, they're going to pay back $74,000 in interest. When the loan is paid off, they will have paid back to the bank $109,000.

The bank is selling this note because this owner is not making their payments. The owner hasn't paid in 17 months, and they owe more than $40,000 to the bank. They are behind $7,724.14, plus the original $35,000. You can buy the note for $10,000. Should you? Let's say you believe you can get that person to start making payments.

They may not be able to pay $454.42 a month, but maybe they can pay $300. So, is this a good investment? Multiply $300 by 12, and this

TRUTH-IN-LENDING DISCLOSURE STATEMENT

ANNUAL PERCENTAGE RATE The cost of your credit as a yearly rate.	FINANCE CHARGE The dollar amount the credit will cost you.	Amount Financed The amount of credit provided to you or on your behalf.	Total of Payments The amount you will have paid after you have made all payments as scheduled.
14.75 %	$ 74,061.84	$ 35,000	$ 109,061

PAYMENT SCHEDULE:

NUMBER OF PAYMENTS	AMOUNT OF PAYMENTS	PAYMENTS ARE DUE monthly BEGINNING	NUMBER OF PAYMENTS	AMOUNT OF PAYMENTS	PAYMENTS ARE DUE monthly BEGINNING
240	$454.42				

**Bank was owed $40,000
I bought the note for $10,000**

will give you your annual profit. You will make $3,600 a year. If you purchased the note for $10,000, then in three years, you will have your money back.

But is that a good deal? To calculate your return on investment, you divide your annual profit by your total investment. In this case, $3,600 ÷ $10,000 = .36, or 36%.

In this scenario, you would be getting a 36% return on your money. That's how you build wealth. That's why buying notes is the most powerful real estate wealth-building system in the world.

FILL-IN-THE BLANKS

(All answers can be found in the answer key that follows)

1. If someone's home is in foreclosure, try to buy the_____.

2. Banks sell notes because_____.

3. Most people base their decisions on_____.

4. Buying a note is a_____to someone's problem.

5. Banks get rich off of_____.

6. To calculate your_____you divide your annual profit by your total investment.

7. People think that_____makes the deal.

8. The most powerful real estate_____ in the world is to buy notes.

9. You've got to learn how to make your money work_____ instead of you working hard for money.

BONUS

Who is your ideal customer? *(Circle the correct answer)*

1. If you don't have any money, you are to buy real estate.

    a. Qualified

    b. Never going

    c. Too poor

    d. Unprepared

2. KPI stands for_____.

    a. Key projection indicator

    b. Key projection index

    c. Key performance indicator

    d. Key performance index

3. Your_____makes you money.

    a. Education

    b. Knowledge

    c. Experience

    d. All of the above

4. ROI stands for_____.

    a. Requisition of inventory

    b. Return on investment

    c. Refund of investment

    d. Return of inventory

5. As an investor, your job is to _____your money.

    a. Multiply

    b. Increase

    c. Grow

    d. All of the above

(Circle the correct answer)

6. *True or False:* Most people are good at analyzing data and making financial choices.

    a. True

    b. False

7. Money doesn't make the deal, _____ make the deal.

    a. Investors

    b. You

    c. Homeowners

    d. Banks

8. You buy a note for $15,000. The owner pays $400/month. What is your annual return?

    a. $4,000

    b. $19,800

    c. $4,800

    d. $10,200

9. Using the same numbers as above, what is your ROI?

    a. 1.32%

    b. 3.2%

    c. 32%

    d. 125%

10. True or False: Some people will give their houses away.

    a. True

    b. False

ANSWER KEY

FILL-IN-THE-BLANKS

1. Note

2. Customers aren't making payments

3. Emotions

4. Solution

5. Notes

6. Return on investment

7. Money

8. Investment strategy

9. Hard for you

QUIZ

1. A
2. C
3. D
4. B
5. D
6. B
7. B
8. C
9. C
10. A

*Homeownership is the principal source
of wealth creation for most people.*

*When the majority of people think about real
estate, they think about the physical structure
(the house) and not the note (the paper).*

—Terry Bontemps

Learn how to make money, build wealth, and be a real estate millionaire. Teach your kids and teens about money, finance, and investing. Download Terry's mobile app Bank Foreclosure Millionaire from Amazon or Apple Store today, $19.99.

Chapter 6 Takeaways And Actionable Steps
For You To Take

Chapter 6: Focuses on the role of an investor in multiplying money, increasing cash flow, and building generational wealth. Here are the key takeaways from this chapter:

1. **Importance of Multiplying Money**: The chapter emphasizes the need to multiply money through smart investment decisions. By understanding key performance indicators (KPIs) such as total profit, return on investment, and profit margin percentage, investors can identify opportunities to maximize their returns.

2. **Increasing Cash Flow**: The chapter highlights the significance of increasing cash flow through real estate investments. By analyzing KPIs such as rental income and expenses, investors can identify properties that generate positive cash flow and contribute to long-term financial stability.

3. **Building Generational Wealth**: The chapter emphasizes the importance of building generational wealth through real estate investments. By acquiring properties and holding them for the long term, investors can create a legacy that can be passed down to future generations.

4. **Actionable Items:** The chapter provides several actionable items that readers can apply immediately, including:

   - Educate yourself on key performance indicators (KPIs) and how they can guide investment decisions.

   - Evaluate potential investment opportunities based on KPIs such as total profit, return on investment, and profit margin percentage.

   - Focus on properties that generate positive cash flow to increase your monthly income.

- Consider long-term investment strategies that can build generational wealth, such as acquiring rental properties.

Overall, the chapter emphasizes the importance of strategic investment decisions, cash flow management, and long-term wealth-building strategies in real estate investing. By applying the actionable items provided, readers can start taking steps towards multiplying their money, increasing cash flow, and building generational wealth.

CHAPTER 7:
KEY PERFORMANCE
INDICATORS

TERRY BONTEMPS' UNPRECEDENTED DATA-DRIVEN
METHODOLOGY TEACHES MEN AND WOMEN HOW TO BUILD
LASTING WEALTH INVESTING IN REAL ESTATE...
COLLAPSING TIME AROUND MULTIPLYING THEIR MONEY,
PROFIT MARGINS, AND RETURN ON INVESTMENT FASTER
THAN ANY OTHER WEALTH-BUILDING INVESTMENT VEHICLE.

A disciplined investment process can give you confidence and peace of mind so you don't get overwhelmed and panic when making financial decisions.

—Terry Bontemps

- **The key performance indicators (KPIs)**
- **The financial numbers**
- **The analytics**
- **The data**

The power of making data-driven decisions to increase your cash flow, multiply your money, and reduce your risk of loss is critical to your financial success. These are the timeless principles that my clients and I have been using since 2001.

You need a disciplined investment process and a proven framework that guides your investment decisions. The nine-question checklist is the exact framework I've used to make smarter investment decisions. It's the exact process I use to evaluate every single real estate deal that I have an interest in. This checklist is based on my 42+ years of experience as a real estate investor.

A disciplined investment process can give you confidence and peace of mind so you don't get overwhelmed and panic when making financial decisions. Answering these nine questions before investing will guide you in selecting profitable investment opportunities.

Let's talk about analytics, one of my favorite subjects, and how you can take 99% of the guesswork out of investing, and how you can have an accurate projection of your potential profits. It's all numbers – real estate is math! If you don't know your numbers, you don't know your real estate investing business. You have to know your key performance indicators. The key performance indicators are the exact money multipliers I use myself to teach my clients to help them make money and build wealth investing in real estate. If you want to financially educate your children about investing and handling their money, teach them the key performance indicators.

They will learn more about managing money, taking investment risks, and making financial decisions just by learning these proven wealth-building formulas. Education in financial matters is more crucial now than ever.

Income is income, and money is money. We make income, and we earn income. People make a lot of money, but they have no wealth. Wealth is created through investing.

Making money and having wealth are two totally different things. You can have a lot of income and still be broke. You have to have this strong desire to learn this thing called investing, which is learning how to multiply your money without working for money.

There are nine different categories from 15 deals that I'm going to be teaching you about in regard to the KPIs, which are:

1. total profit
2. total investment
3. return on investment
4. time to get investment back
5. payback period
6. profit margin %
7. equity
8. buying real estate on the dollar
9. multiplied and increased investment.

I've broken down 15 different deals into nine categories of a house to help us analyze our real estate investment profit potential. Nine different slices or ways to look at how we base our decisions when investing in real estate. The reason I did this is so we can scale our real estate investing business. This is very powerful.

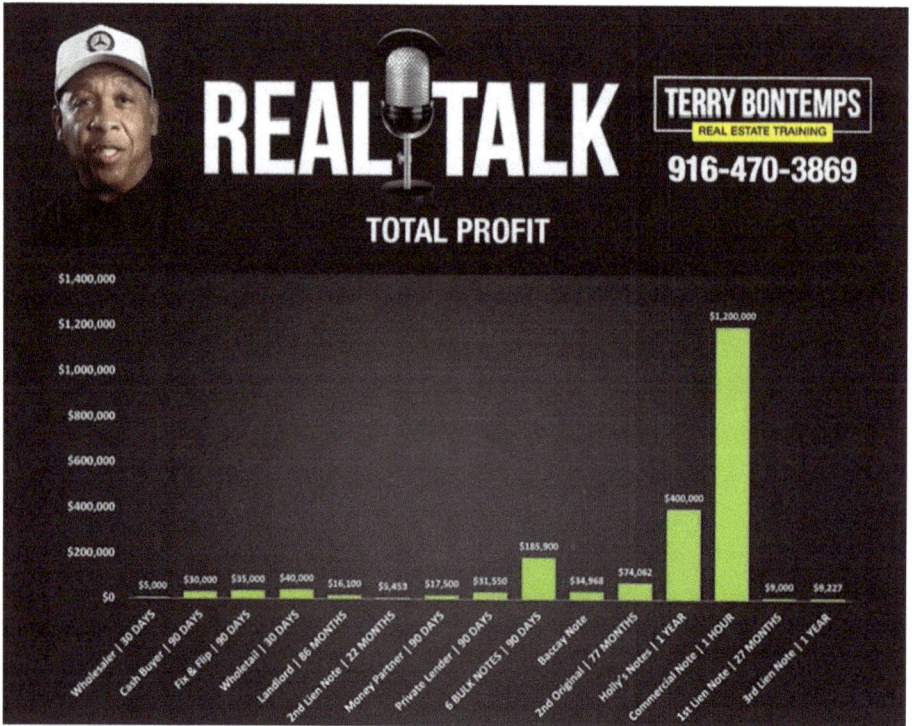

REAL TALK

TERRY BONTEMPS
REAL ESTATE TRAINING
916-470-3869

TOTAL PROFIT

The first key performance indicator is total profit. My student Ron is the one who skyrockets to the top on the right. He made $1.2 million on a commercial note that he bought from a bank in one hour. The numbers for a wholesaler, fix and flipper, and landlord are at the far-left end. On the right side, that's note buying – buying the paper or mortgage. Purchasing a property from the seller is represented on the left side of the diagram.

I want you to pay close attention to the four areas to the right. Take a look at Holly's note deal. She made a $400,000 profit on one deal she bought from a bank.

Next to Holly's deal is Ron's commercial note deal. Move two spots, and you'll see a note that I bought. It was a third mortgage that I bought from a bank. It was the first note I ever bought. Moreover, I had no idea what I was doing when I bought it. My profit was $9,227.

138

Go to the left; you will see six notes I bought in bulk. I made $185,900 on those deals.

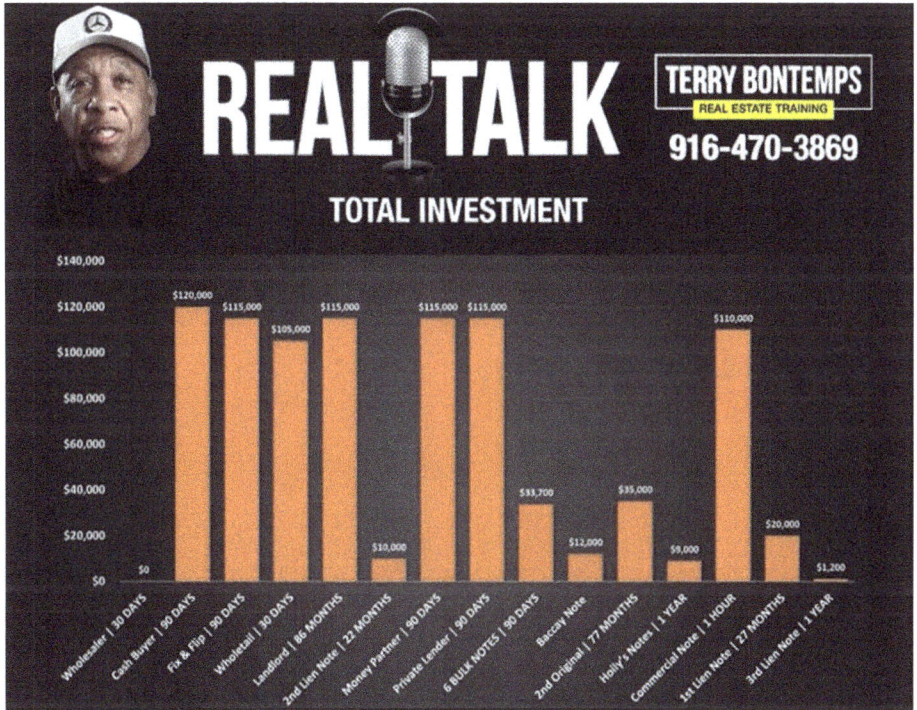

The next key performance indicator is total investment. These charts that you're seeing are from different deals of what my students and I had to invest in making the profits we've made. These are the analytics, the data, the metrics, the numbers, and the math.

Go to Holly's deal at the far right. She invested $9,000 to make $400,000.

Ron invested $110,000 to buy his commercial note from the bank to make $1.2 million.

I invested $1,200 to buy my note from the bank to make $9,227. To buy six notes from the bank, I invested $33,700 to make $186,700 in profits. To the far left, the cash buyer invested $120,000 to make a $30,000 profit. The cash buyer fixed the property, hired contractors, staged it, and sold it using a realtor. The fix and flipper invested $115,000 to make a $35,000 profit after rehabbing and selling the property. You'll see that the cash buyer and the fix and flipper invested a lot of money in comparison to their investment and their profit. In other words, the numbers say the cash buyer, and fix and flipper invested a lot of money to make a small profit. If you look to the right at the note buyers, they invested a small amount in comparison to make a large profit. This is the benefit of learning how to analyze real estate deals using the key performance indicators.

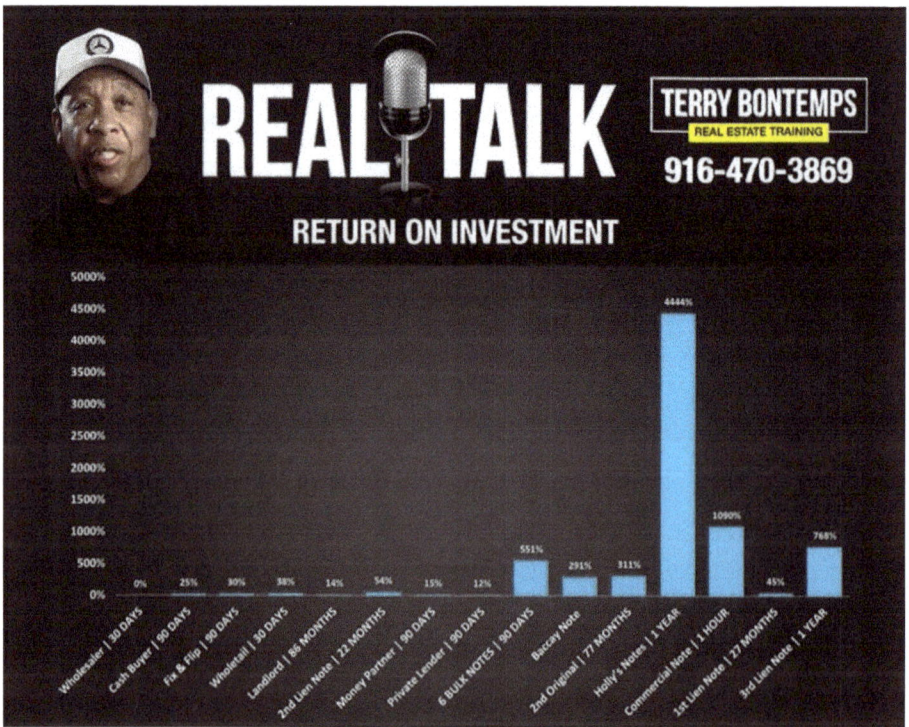

My favorite KPI is the return on investment. Again, if you look to the far right, the high side with the highest graph is my student, Holly. That's a 4444% return on her investment that you see at the top of the chart. Holly bought a note for $9,000 and made a $400,000 profit from one deal.

At the opposite end, where there's hardly any graph, that's the wholesaler, fix and flipper, and landlord. There's hardly anything on the graph compared to the return on investment for note buying. This is the analytics and what the data is telling us.

Return on investment is the profit compared to the investment, and it's based on a percentage. Holly's ROI is 4444%. Here's the math behind her incredible return on investment. You take the profit and divide it by the investment. Holly invested $9,000, and her profit was $400,000. $400,000 divided by $9,000 = 44.44. You multiply 44.44 x 100, which moves the decimal two places to the right, which gives her a 4444% return on her investment (ROI). WOW!

Ron made a 1090% ROI. He invested $110,000 and made $1.2 million. You take the profit and divide it by the investment. Ron invested $110,000, and his profit was $1.2 million. $1.2 million divided by $110,000 = 10.90. You multiply 10.90 x 100, which moves the decimal two places to the right, which gives him a 1090% return on his investment. WOW!

I made a 768% ROI for the note I purchased for $1,200 and made $9,227. My ROI is 551% for the six notes that I purchased. I purchased the six notes for $33,700 and made $185,900.

Do the math, and put the numbers in your calculator to learn how to multiply your money and build wealth for you and your family. Let's look at the left side – the cash buyer and the fix and flipper's return on investment. The cash buyers' ROI is 25%, and the cash buyer invested $120,000 and made a $30,000 profit.

The fix and flipper invested $115,000 and made a $35,000 profit for a 30.43% ROI.

Look at the difference in ROI from the house flippers compared to buying the note and being the bank. These are the key performance indicators and graphs to track the results of your investments.

How can you compare one deal against another deal? What deals do you want to spend your time on, and which deal is more profitable for you? It's a nice crystal ball into your finances when you can see the numbers using the key performance indicators. That's what I love about the KPIs.

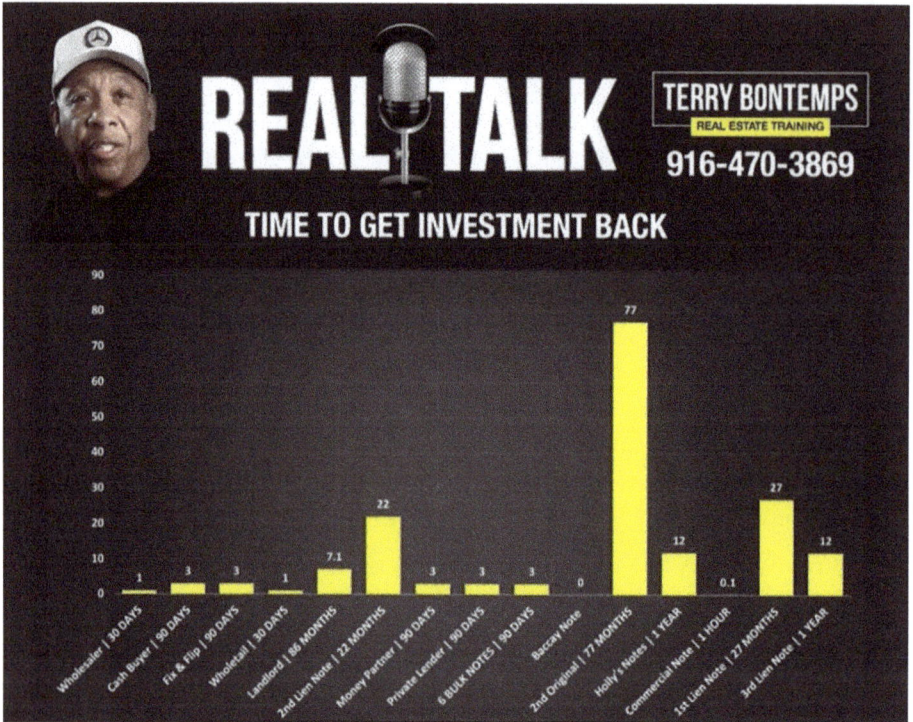

The next KPI is the actual time it took for us to get our investment back. On the right side of the chart, I bought a third note for $1,227. It took me one year to get my $9,227 profit check.

Ron invested $110,000, and it took him one hour to complete his $1.2 million dollar deal with the bank. It took Holly nine months to make a profit of $400,000 from her $9,000 investment.

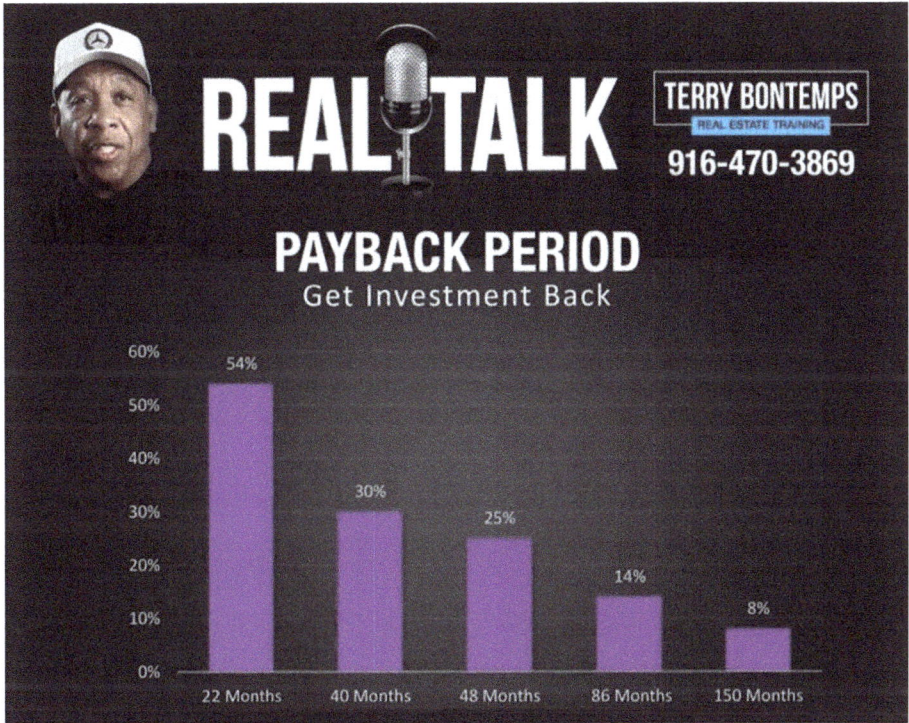

REAL TALK

TERRY BONTEMPS
REAL ESTATE TRAINING
916-470-3869

PAYBACK PERIOD
Get Investment Back

I've tracked the data. I've studied. I know how to multiply my money as an investor. I've done the research. And to give you a little bit more detail, if I invest my money or you invest your money at 54%, no matter how much money it is, whether it's $1, $100, $1,000, $1 million dollars, or $10 million, whether you're buying in Dubai or any other country – **NO MATTER HOW MUCH MONEY YOU INVEST**, your investment will come back in 22 months.

If I invest my money or you invest yours, and it earns a 14% return on your investment, **NO MATTER HOW MUCH MONEY YOU INVEST**, your investment will come back in 86 months, and every dollar invested will make a 14-cent profit from a 14% return on the investment.

If I invest my money or you invest your money, and it earns a 25% return on your investment, **NO MATTER HOW MUCH MONEY YOU INVEST**, your investment will come back in 48 months, and every dollar invested will make a 25-cent profit from a 25% return on the investment.

If I invest my money or you invest your money, and it earns a 30% return on your investment, **NO MATTER HOW MUCH MONEY YOU INVEST**, your investment will come back in 40 months, and every dollar invested will make a 30-cent profit from a 30% return on the investment.

I talked about investing $10,000 of my own money to buy a note from a bank. I knew that I wanted a 54% return on my investment. I also knew that if I was getting a 54% return on my investment and if I could get the homeowners to make their $454.42 monthly payment, I would get my $10,000 back in 22 months, and every dollar I invested will make a 54-cent profit when I earn a 54% return on my investment.

Can you guys see the high financial intelligence that I'm going to be transferring to you when you become one of my real estate coaching students? And this is one-on-one training that I will be offering you.

So, what are you earning from your bank on your savings account? What are you getting from that savings account? The bank is giving you 1%, 2%, or 3%. Guess what?

Everybody needs a better investment vehicle so they can build wealth. You need to be earning better than 1%, 2%, or 3% on your money.

All other real estate programs teach you how to wholesale houses, fix them up and flip them, or how to be a landlord. Nobody is teaching you how to be the bank. Nobody is teaching you how to make money just like the banks do.

In order to build wealth, you must know how wealth is built, and the predominant way wealth is built is by owning real estate. When you invest your money, you need to know what return you want to earn on your investment and the amount of time it will take you to get your money back.

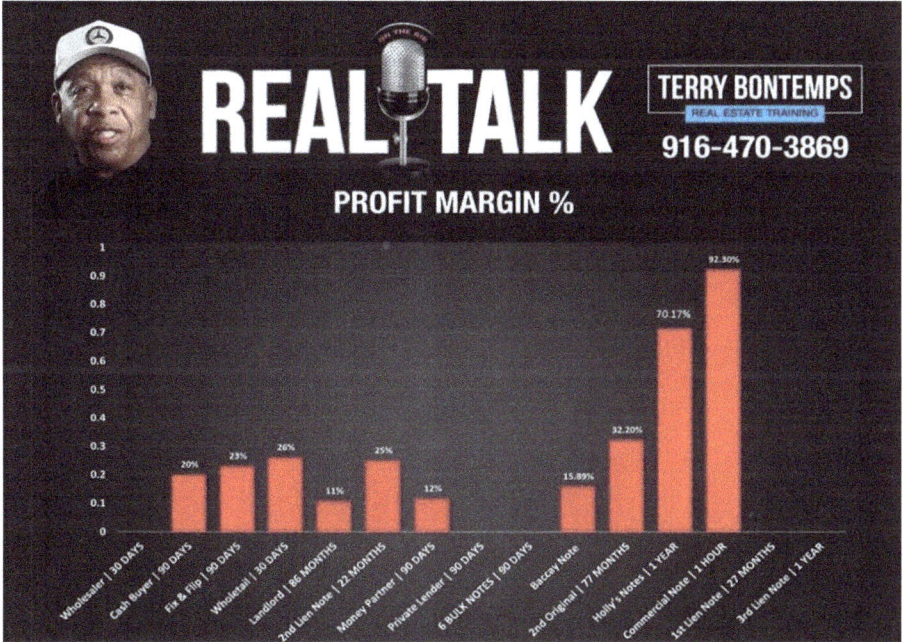

REAL TALK

TERRY BONTEMPS
REAL ESTATE TRAINING
916-470-3869

PROFIT MARGIN %

The next KPI is the profit margin percentage. How much of the deal based on a percentage is your actual profit minus expenses? Again, the highest returns are from my students who are buying notes. The highest one is 92.30%. That was Ron's deal. He made $1.2 million in one hour by buying a commercial note from a bank. He invested $110,000 to make $1.2 million, so you can see that 92.30% of that deal was pure profit. I love the analytics!

To calculate the profit margin percentage, you divide the profit by the value of the property. Next, you multiply your answer by 100. The value of the commercial property was $1.3 million, and $1.2 million divided by $1.3 million = .9230 .9230 x 100 = 92.30%

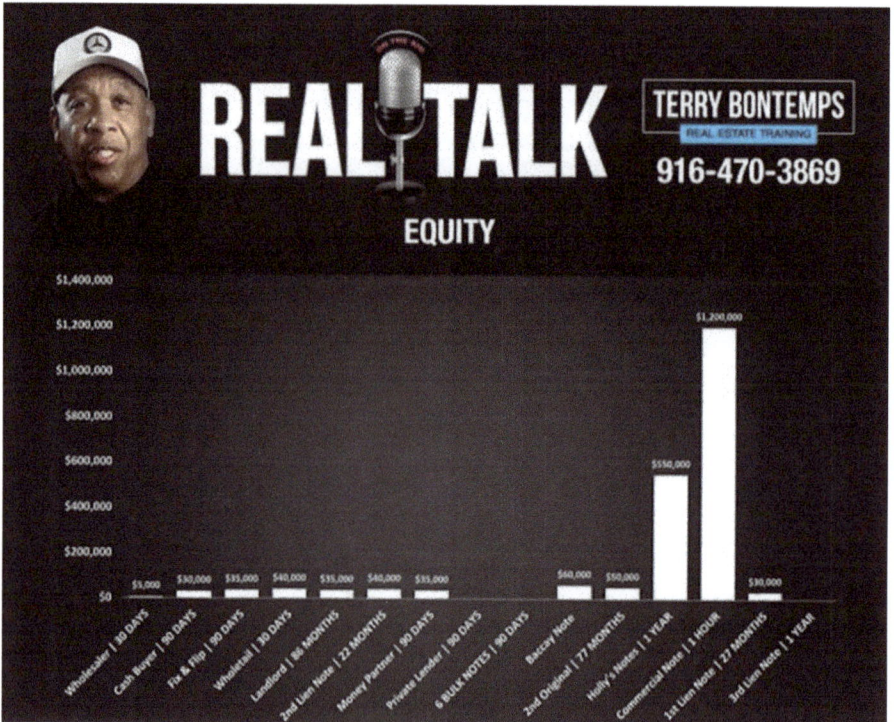

REAL TALK

TERRY BONTEMPS
REAL ESTATE TRAINING
916-470-3869

EQUITY

The next KPI is equity. Does the deal have any equity? Equity in the property is important because it's one way to gauge the safety of not losing your investment. Equity is a type of cushion or protection. I'm talking about key performance indicators. The numbers that determine when you invest your money will it be a deal or not a deal. These KPIs must be considered when making real estate investments because they will indicate whether a bargain exists.

What do most people do? They use emotions to make their financial decisions. They cannot analyze whether a real estate deal will make them money or lose them money. They're using no logic to make smarter investment decisions, and they wonder why they lose money.

The higher your equity position the less chance you have of losing your investment. The lower your equity position, the higher your chances of losing your investment.

The formula for calculating equity is the total debt minus the market value of the property. Ron invested $110,000. The property was worth $1.3 million. That leaves $1.2 million in equity.

The next KPI is what are you buying real estate on the dollar for. The right side is the bank side which is buying the note, and the right side is buying the property. On the left side, look at how much the wholesaler, fix and flipper, and landlord are paying on the dollar to own real estate.

I mentioned earlier about buying a note from the bank for $10,000. It was owed $40,000. I bought that note for 25 cents on the dollar. At the far right, look at the purchase price on the dollar. My students have bought for 18 cents on the dollar, 34 cents, 47 cents, 2 cents, 9 cents, 45 cents, and 13 cents for controlling real estate.

When you're purchasing real estate for pennies on the dollar that leaves a whole lot of room to make bigger profits. This is how as an investor, you can multiply your money, increase your cash flow, and build generational wealth.

The higher you spend on the dollar for real estate, the less profits you will make. The fix and flipper spent 76 cents on the dollar to buy real estate, which includes repairs and closing costs. That leaves only 24 cents of profit for every dollar invested for the fix and flipper.

Holly spent 2 cents on the dollar to buy real estate with no repairs and closing costs buying notes.

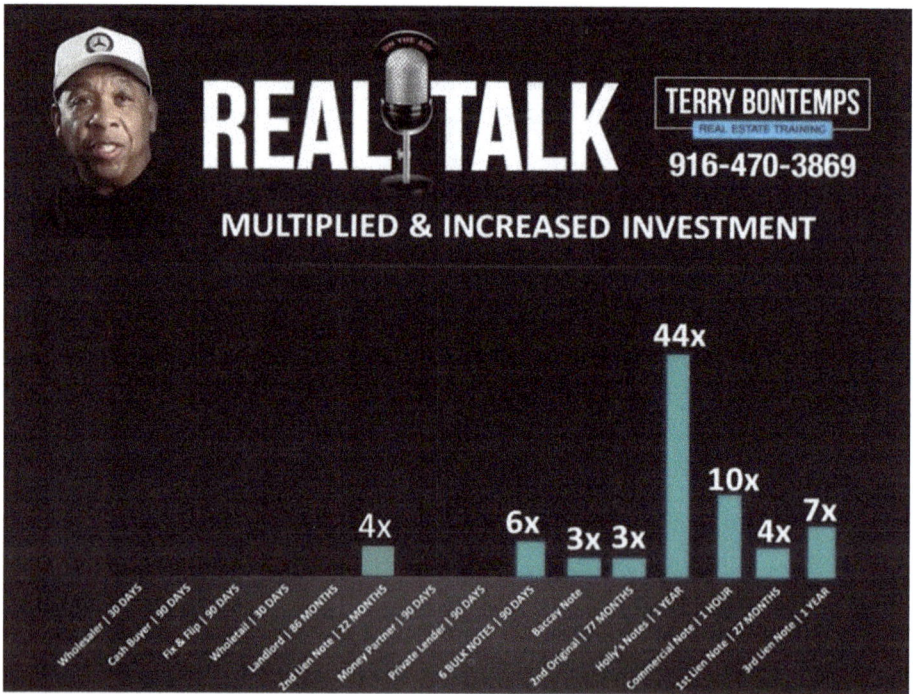

The next KPI is multiplying and increased investment. I've measured the multiples of money made on our real estate deals compared to our investment amounts, and you can see our results with this graph.

Take a look at the 44 times multiple, which is Holly's deal. She invested $9,000 to buy notes from a bank, and her profit was $400,000. That's a 44 times multiple of her money. WOW, that's impressive! You don't get wealthy working for money, you get wealthy by multiplying your money.

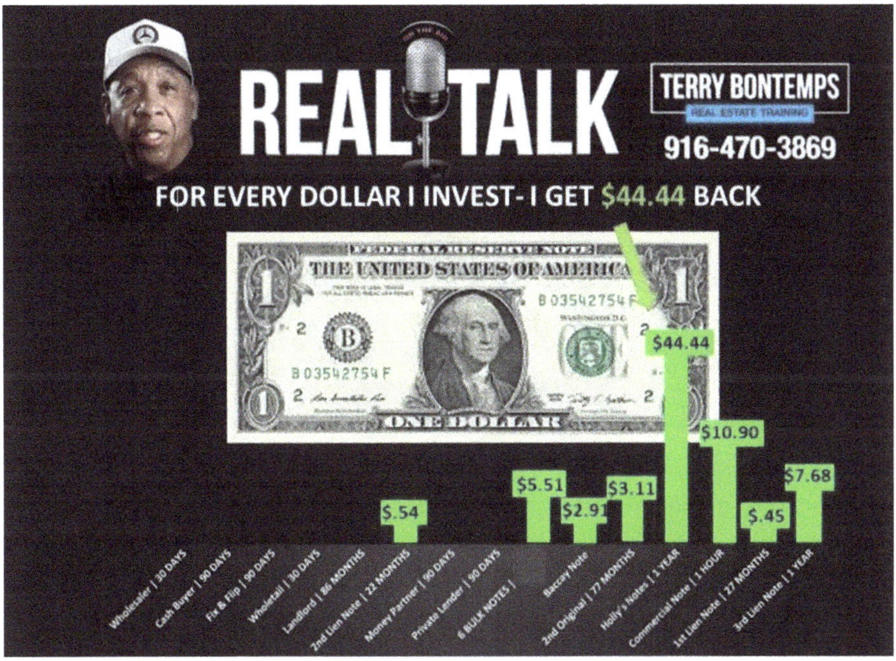

For Every Dollar I Invest - I Get $44.44 Back

LET ME GIVE YOU ANOTHER WEALTH BUILDING SECRET. THIS WILL BLOW YOUR MIND! The amount of money you'll make for every dollar you invest...

For every dollar Holly invested on this deal, she will make $44.44 of profit ... think about that, it's powerful. She made $400,000 as her profit. She invested $9,000 of her own money to do the deal. Put $400,000 in your calculator and divide it by $9,000 which equals $44.44. Do the math and put the numbers in your calculator.

Let me give you why this KPI is so significant for you when building wealth and investing in real estate. Let's reverse engineer this KPI. **Before you put your money into any real estate deal ask yourself how much money do you want to make for every dollar you invest?** Use your amount as a guide along with the other KPIs to make your final decision as to whether you should do the deal or not.

Let's look at the various amounts on the dollar that other students of mine that have invested in real estate. See the KPI graph above.

149

On the left side at the 2nd lien note/22 months. For every dollar invested on this deal, **$.54 cents of profit will be made**…

Moving right, the 6 note deals. For every dollar invested on this deal, **$5.51 of profits will be made**…

The Baccay note. For every dollar invested **$2.91 of profits will be made**…

2nd original/77 months. For every dollar invested **$3.11 of profits will be made**…

Holly's note. For every dollar invested **$44.44 of profits will be made**…

Commercial note. For every dollar invested **$10.90 of profits will be made**…

1st lien note/27 months… For every dollar invested **$.45 cents of profits will be made**… 3rd lien note/1 year… For every dollar invested **$7.68 of profits will be made**…

Look to the left; the wholesaler, fix and flipper, and landlord aren't multiplying their money as much as note buyers are, and their returns are not even on the chart. Again, this is why banks have become the richest institutions in the world and why note buying is the most powerful real estate wealth-building strategy ever developed.

Click the link below or scan QR code to view video of Terry demonstrating the key performance indicators
https://www.youtube.com/watch?v=VbQVEHn8LZo

**IF YOU DON'T UNDERSTAND MONEY,
YOU'LL SPEND YOUR LIFE
WORKING FOR SOMEONE WHO DOES**

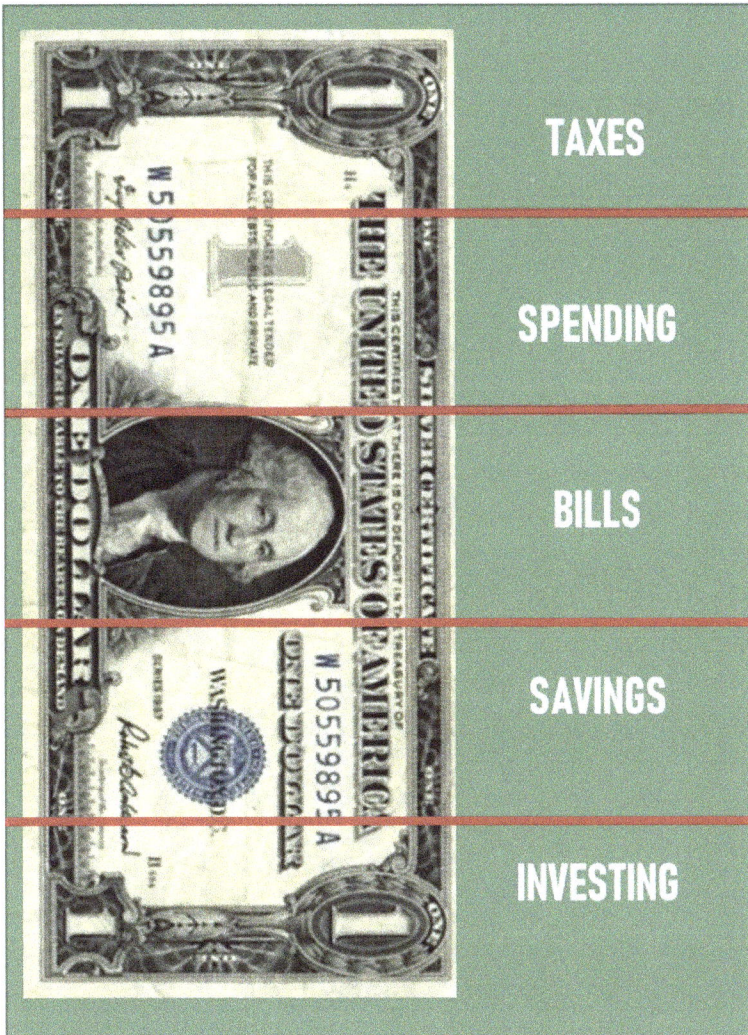

TAXES

SPENDING

BILLS

SAVINGS

INVESTING

Only 5 Things You Can Do With Your Money

What are you doing with your money? Are you spending everything you make on bills? We all are paying our fair share of taxes. Invest in your financial education so you can learn how to multiply your money, increase your cash flow, and build generational wealth for you and your family.

*I want you to put the numbers in your calculator
so you can actually see the money, cash flow,
and wealth you could be generating when you
know the key performance indicators.*

—Terry Bontemps

Chapter 7 Takeaways and Actionable Steps
For You To Take

Chapter 7: Discusses key performance indicators (KPIs) in real estate investing. Here are the key takeaways and actionable items from this chapter:

1. **Importance of KPIs**: The chapter emphasizes the importance of using data-driven decision-making in real estate investing. KPIs provide a clear understanding of the potential profitability of a real estate investment and help investors evaluate the financial viability of a deal.

2. **Evaluating Profitability**: KPIs such as total profit, return on investment (ROI), profit margin percentage, and multiplied and increased investment help investors evaluate the profitability of a real estate deal. Investors should analyze these KPIs to determine if a deal is worth pursuing.

3. **Comparing Investment Opportunities**: KPIs allow investors to compare different investment opportunities and identify the deals that offer the highest potential returns. By analyzing KPIs such as total profit, ROI, and profit margin percentage, investors can make informed decisions about which deals to pursue.

4. **Assessing Risk**: KPIs such as equity and buying real estate on the dollar help investors assess the risk associated with a real estate investment. By analyzing these KPIs, investors can determine the level of risk involved in a deal and make informed decisions.

5. **Setting Investment Goals**: KPIs provide a benchmark for setting investment goals. By analyzing KPIs such as ROI and multiplied and increased investment, investors can set specific targets for their real estate investments and track their progress towards achieving those goals.

6. **Making Informed Decisions**: KPIs provide data-driven insights that help investors make informed decisions. By analyzing KPIs such as total profit, ROI, and profit margin percentage, investors can evaluate the financial viability of a real estate investment and make decisions based on objective data rather than emotions or assumptions.

Overall, the key takeaway from this chapter is that using KPIs in real estate investing is essential for evaluating profitability, comparing investment opportunities, assessing risk, setting investment goals, and making informed decisions. Investors should analyze KPIs to determine the potential profitability of a deal and make informed decisions based on objective data.

CHAPTER 8:
MY STUDENTS HAVE BECOME MILLIONAIRES AND MULTI-MILLIONAIRES FROM WHAT I'VE TAUGHT THEM ABOUT BEING THE BANK

When you invest your money, you should know what your investment will be, how much your profit is, when you will get your investment back, what multiple on your money you will be earning, what your ROI is, what your profit margin % is, how much on the dollar you're buying for, and if the property has any equity. These are the Key Performance Indicators.

—Terry Bontemps

Please grab your calculator, because that is how I will teach you how to invest in real estate. Put $1 million in your calculator.

When you put the numbers in the calculator, you can see how you multiply your money and how wealth is built. Return to this training over, and over, and over again to re-learn, and practice what I've been teaching you. This is how you earn your finance degree in building wealth.

You learn by inputting the numbers in the calculator so you can see how the numbers and formulas work. Now you have a model to work from that you can use when you invest your money in the future. So, grab your calculator, put a million in there, and just let it sit.

Before you invest in real estate or any other investment, you should be able to answer the majority of the following eight questions. I will use the financial numbers from the deal I invested $10,000 in and made a $40,000 profit for you to learn from.

1. You should know how much your profit is: $40,000

2. You should know how much your investment is: $10,000

3. You should know your return on investment: 400%

4. You should know how long it will take to receive your investment back: (unknown)

5. You should know your profit margin percentage: (unknown)

6. You should know if the property has any equity or not: $50,000

7. You should know the price you are buying real estate for on the dollar: 25 cents?

8. You should know what multiple you are earning on your investment: 4 times (for every dollar I invest, I will make $4 of profit)

REHABBER VS NOTES

Terry Bontemps Students Are Making The Most Money Per Deal Currently in The U.S

	PROFIT	$400,000
$35,000	INVESTMENT	$9,000
$115,OOO	RETURN ON INVESTMENT	4444%
30.4%	TIME TO GET INVESTMENT BACK	9 Months
60-90 Days	PROFIT MARGIN %	70.1%
23.3%	EQUITY	$170,000
$35,000	BUYING FOR ON THE DOLLAR	.02 cents
.76 cents		

REHABBER VS NOTES

Terry Bontemps Students Are Making The Most Money Per Deal Currently in The U.S

N/A	MULTIPLIED & INCREASED INVESTMENT x TIMES	44X

I want to compare a fix-and-flip deal and what my student Holly did on her deal. I showed you the key performance indicators in the previous chapter, which were:

- Profit
- Investment
- Return on investment
- Time to get investment back
- Profit margin %
- Equity
- Buying real estate on the dollar
- Multiplied and increased investment

The key performance indicators are in order below, so that you can see what this financial projection means about doing the analytics from the data I've collected from our past deals. Let's take a look.

LET'S COMPARE THE DATA FROM EACH DEAL

- The rehabber makes a $35,000 profit
- They invest $115,000
- Their return on investment is 30.4%
- The time to get the investment back is 60 to 90 days
- Their profit margin is 23%
- There is $35,000 of equity.

Equity is the discrepancy between a property's market worth and outstanding debt. The rehabber borrowed $115,000 from a bank to finance the property in this deal. The repaired value of the property is $150,000. The difference between the two is $35,000

- Rehabber buys real estate for 76 cents on the dollar.

The rehabber doesn't multiply and increase their investment The rehabber's investment is $115,000, which includes purchase price, repairs, and closing costs. Their profit is $35,000, which means their

159

investment of $115,000 is not multiplying. For every dollar the rehabber invests, they're only making 24 cents of profit.

Let's talk about buying paper, notes, mortgages, and the financing. Let's look at the data and analytics from Holly's deal. Her financial numbers are simply freaking amazing!

- Holly made a $400,000 profit
- She invested $9,000
- Her return on investment is 4444%
- It took Holly nine months to get her investment back
- Holly's profit margin is 70.1%
- There is $170,000 of equity
- She is buying real estate for 2 cents on the dollar
- Holly multiplied her investment by 44 times (for every dollar invested, she'll make $44.44)

MY STUDENTS HAVE BECOME MILLIONAIRES AND MULTI-MILLIONAIRES FROM WHAT I'VE TAUGHT THEM ABOUT BUYING NOTES FROM BANKS

Let's compare Holly's deal to Ron's deal. Again, Ron made $1.2 million in one-hour buying notes, and Holly made $400,000 in nine months. So, what is the comparison between the two? Which deal has the best analytics? If I were to ask you guys, who would you choose if you had a choice? You obviously would say to me, "Terry, I'll take both of them. I'll take Ron's $1.2 million because that's a lot. I'll even take Holly's $400,000."

That's simply amazing! And again, how did these guys do this? I taught them how to invest in notes. Holly paid $25,000 for her education. She went to a seminar. The seminar told her, "Hey, look, if you pay us $25,000, we have this fantastic, great guy, great personality, coolest guy in the world named Terry Bontemps who will come to your town and teach you for three days how to make money investing in real estate." That's what Holly did.

Ron went to the bank to buy his commercial note. He walked into the bank and said, "Hey, I would like to buy this property over here." The bank says, "We can't sell it. We can't sell it because we don't own it, but we will sell you the note".

So, what does Ron do? Ron thinks, "Man, I have no idea what notes are." He gets on the internet, and he starts surfing YouTube videos. Guess who he finds? He finds some great guy with a great personality and a great smile, who has been involved in real estate for over 42 years and has been teaching people for 19 years. He's got over 400 videos on YouTube. His name is Terry Bontemps. And guess what? He calls me.

"Hey, this is Terry. How can I help you? Yeah, you got a bank that wants to sell you a note, huh? Alright. You want to go in and buy the note on Tuesday. Today is Friday, and you want me to train you?"

I said, "Okay, I'll tell you what to do. I'll charge you $700 for a Saturday and Sunday. I trained Ron for two days. He goes into the bank on Tuesday. The bank was owed $850,000 for a note. The property was worth $1.3 million. The bank was asking $300,000 for the note. My student Ron offered $110,000 and gave them the cash. One hour of work, and he made $1.2 million from that transaction.

Let's compare the data and the numbers for Ron's and Holly's deal.

- Ron made $1.2 million on his deal
- He invested $110,000
- His return on investment is 1090%
- The time to get the investment back is one hour
- His profit margin percentage is 70.1%
- There is $1.2 million of equity
- Ron is buying real estate for 9 cents on the dollar
- Ron is multiplying and increasing his investment by 10 times ($10.90 profit for every dollar he invested)

- Holly made a $400,000 profit
- She invested $9,000
- Her return on investment is 4444%
- It took Holly nine months to get her investment back
- Holly's profit margin is 70.1%
- There is $170,000 of equity
- She is buying real estate for 2 cents on the dollar
- Holly multiplied her investment by 44 times ($44.44 of profit for every dollar she invested)

That's how you make money, build generational wealth and become a millionaire investing in real estate. That's exactly how you multiply your money and increase your cash flow. I've asked you guys to get your calculators so I can teach you how to be a real estate investor. You go to seminars and are often on webinars, sitting there bored. The speaker is talking, and you're dozing off. And after so many times of hearing so much stuff, even when you're reading, you don't retain it. You're not able to implement what you've been taught so you can change your financial destiny.

Key performance indicators (KPIs) can be used to analyze potential real estate deals by evaluating the financial viability, profitability, and risk associated with the investment. By analyzing these KPIs, investors can make informed financial decisions, compare different investment opportunities, and assess the potential return on investment.

HOW MUCH IS YOUR INVESTMENT
$9,000

MULTIPLIED INVESTMENT
44X

HOW MUCH IS YOUR PROFIT
$400,000

TIME TO GET BACK INVESTMENT
9 months

PROFIT MARGIN %
70.1%

BUYING REAL ESTATE ON THE $1
.02 cents on the dollar

WHAT'S YOUR ROI
4444%

EQUITY
$170,000

EVERY $1 INVESTED WILL MAKE
$44.44

PAYBACK PERIOD (cash flow)
N/A

By evaluating Ron' and Holly's KPIs, investors can assess the potential profitability of a real estate investment, compare different opportunities, assess risk, set investment goals, and make informed decisions.

HOW MUCH IS YOUR INVESTMENT $110,000	MULTIPLIED INVESTMENT 11X
HOW MUCH IS YOUR PROFIT $1.2 million	TIME TO GET BACK INVESTMENT N/A
PROFIT MARGIN % 92.3%	BUYING REAL ESTATE ON THE $1 .09 cents on the dollar
WHAT'S YOUR ROI 1090%	EQUITY $1.2 million
EVERY $1 INVESTED WILL MAKE $10.90	PAYBACK PERIOD (cash flow) N/A

If I have you participate by using your calculator, then you will retain the information that I'm trying to teach you. I want you to put in your calculator $1 million, put that in your calculator. That $1 million is symbolic of your worth, the amount of money you will have in your bank account, the value of your home that you will live in or the amount of inheritance you will leave each one of your children.

Participate and play all out! **Take a look at the next page where I show you the KPI's for 174 notes that I tried to flip to a hedge fund.**

According to your latest financial numbers, if you retired today, you could live very, very comfortably until about 2 p.m. tomorrow

WHAT DO YOUR NUMBERS SAY ABOUT YOUR FINANCES?

KEY PERFORMANCE INDICATORS

174 1st LOANS FLIP TO HEDGE FUND

Terry Bontemps Students Are Making The Most Money Per Deal Currently in The U.S

Value		Indicator
$40 MILLION		ARV
$22 MILLION		OFFER TO BANK
.55 cents		BUYING ON THE DOLLAR
81%		RETURN ON INVESTMENT
45%		PROFIT MARGIN %
$220,000		FLIP FEE
$127,586		AVERAGE PRICE PER HOUSE

KEY PERFORMANCE INDICATORS

THE POWER OF BUYING 2nd's

Terry Bontemps Students Are Making The Most Money Per Deal Currently in The U.S

Value		Indicator
$185,900		ARV
$33,700		OFFER TO BANK
5.5 cents		BUYING ON THE DOLLAR
551%		RETURN ON INVESTMENT
$30,983		AVERAGE PROFIT PER NOTE
		FLIP FEE
		PROFIT MARGIN %

167

Click the link below or scan QR code to view video of Terry demonstrating the key performance indicators
https://www.youtube.com/watch?v=1dpNgQjycZI

There are way too many people who believe you need money, good credit and experience to start investing in real estate and it's simply NOT TRUE! So many deserving people have been locked out of the WEALTH BUILDING EXPERIENCE due to simply believing the myths and conventional thinking of realtors, bankers and financial institutions.

—Terry Bontemps

Learn how to make money, build wealth, and be a real estate millionaire. Teach your kids and teens about money, finance, and investing. Download Terry's mobile app Bank Foreclosure Millionaire from Amazon or Apple Store today, $19.99.

Chapter 8 Takeaways and Actionable Steps For You To Take

Chapter 8: Discusses how Terry Bontemps' students have become millionaires and multi- millionaires by following his teachings on being the bank. The key takeaways from this chapter include:

1. **The Importance Of Buying Notes From Banks**: Terry Bontemps emphasizes the power of buying notes or mortgages from banks as a wealth-building strategy. He shares success stories of his students who have made significant profits by purchasing commercial notes and residential notes.

2. **The Ten Key Performance Indicators (KPIs):** Terry introduces the concept of KPIs in real estate investing. These KPIs include total profit, total investment, return on investment, time to get investment back, payback period, profit margin percentage, equity, buying real estate on the dollar, when you invest a dollar- how much you would make in return plus multiplied and increased investment. Understanding and analyzing these KPIs can guide investors in selecting profitable investment opportunities.

3. **The Power Of Data-Driven Decisions**: He emphasizes the importance of making data- driven decisions in real estate investing. By knowing and analyzing the key performance indicators, investors can increase their cash flow, multiply their money, and reduce the risk of loss.

4. **The Different Investment Categories:** Terry Bontemps breaks down 15 different real estate deals into nine categories based on the key performance indicators. These categories provide a framework for evaluating and comparing investment opportunities.

5. **The Potential For High Returns**: The chapter highlights the significant returns that can be achieved through real estate investing. Examples are given of students who have made profits ranging from $400,000 to $1.2 million on individual deals.

Actionable items for the reader:

1. **Learn About The Key Performance Indicators**: Familiarize yourself with the nine key performance indicators mentioned in the chapter. Understand how they can be used to evaluate real estate deals and guide investment decisions.

2. **Analyze Real Estate Deals Using KPIs**: Apply the knowledge of key performance indicators to analyze potential real estate deals. Consider factors such as total profit, return on investment, and profit margin percentage when evaluating the profitability of an investment opportunity.

3. **Consider Buying Notes**: Explore the possibility of purchasing notes or mortgages from banks as a wealth-building strategy. Research the process and potential benefits of buying notes and learn from success stories of others who have done it.

4. **Seek Education And Mentorship**: Consider seeking education and mentorship from experienced real estate investors like Terry Bontemps. Look for resources, courses, or coaching programs that can provide guidance and support in your real estate investing journey.

5. **Make Data-Driven Decisions**: Embrace the concept of making data-driven decisions in your real estate investing. Use the key performance indicators and other relevant data to guide your investment choices and reduce the risk of financial loss.

6. **Start Small And Scale Up**: Begin with smaller real estate deals and gradually scale up as you gain experience and confidence. Focus on building a solid foundation of knowledge and skills before taking on larger and more complex investments.

7. **Network And Build Relationships**: Connect with other real estate investors, attend industry events, and join online communities to expand your network and learn from others' experiences. Building relationships with like-minded individuals can provide valuable insights and opportunities for collaboration.

8. **Take Action And Be Consistent**: Implement the knowledge and strategies learned from Terry Bontemps and other real estate experts. Take consistent action towards your wealth-building goals and stay committed to your financial success.

CHAPTER 9:
THE MILLIONAIRE'S
WEALTH-BUILDING
GAME

WEALTH HABIT #5:
OWNING REAL ESTATE

THE MILLIONAIRE'S WEALTH-BUILDING GAME

*Do you have what it takes to make money, build
wealth, get rich, and be a real estate millionaire?*

*Do you think you're a millionaire in the making?
Play this wealth-building game to find out if
you are truly destined to be a millionaire.*

*It doesn't matter if you've made millions or you've never
made a dime investing in real estate, this technology
will give you the edge you need to make money and
build wealth in your local real estate market.*

—Terry Bontemps

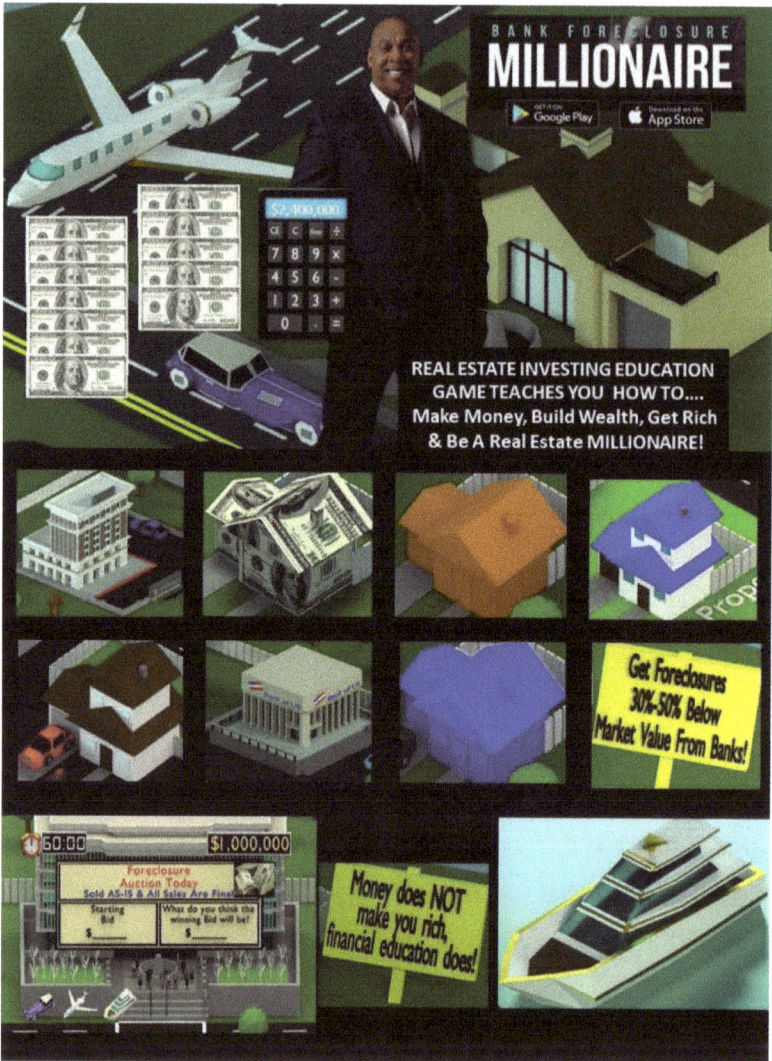

BANK FORECLOSURE MILLIONAIRE

WEALTH-BUILDING REAL ESTATE EDUCATION GAME

Have you ever watched those house flipping shows on television? Have you ever asked yourself, "How do they do it, and how do they make those big profit checks? What do they know in order to buy, sell, rent and flip houses?"

How do they get the money to buy the houses that make them so much money? Have you ever wondered what your life would be like if you were a successful real estate investor?

Have you ever imagined yourself flipping houses and making lots of money just like they do on those HGTV television shows? Now, you can learn how professional investors make hefty profits with my mobile app called Bank Foreclosure Millionaire.

My Bank Foreclosure Millionaire wealth-building real estate investing education game will teach you step-by-step how big money is made buying, renting, selling, and flipping houses.

WEALTH-BUILDING
GAME CONCEPT

A profit-filled financial investment education game in which you learn about money, building wealth, finance, and real estate investment strategies.

The game teaches you the intricate details of what the wealthy know about making money by investing in real estate. Learn the numbers and the skill level necessary for you to become financially independent from buying, renting, selling, flipping, and managing investment properties across the United States.

Learn investment strategies, situations and valuable financial lessons that simulate the real world of real estate investing without putting your own money at risk.

**WEALTH-BUILDING
GAME SUMMARY**

**MAKE AS MUCH MONEY AS FAST
AS YOU CAN IN**

ONE HOUR

**BUYING, SELLING, RENTING,
MANAGING, AND FLIPPING HOUSES
ACROSS THE UNITED STATES
REAL ESTATE MARKET
THROUGH A VARIETY OF PROFITABLE
INVESTMENT STRATEGIES AND
OPPORTUNITIES**

WHAT WILL YOU DO WITH THE PROFITS YOU MAKE FROM YOUR REAL ESTATE?

- Get out of debt?

- Pay off your home?

- Buy your dream car?

- Pay off student loans?

- Take exotic vacations?

- Buy rental property?

- Pay cash for college?

- Donate to your favorite charity?

- Give to your church?

- Care for your parents?

- Reinvest your profits?

- Buy a business?

- Save for retirement?

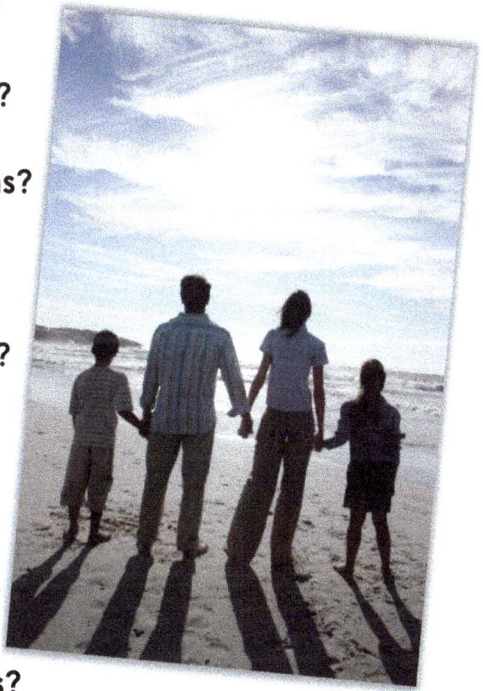

EVERYONE STARTS THE
WEALTH-BUILDING GAME
WITH NO MONEY, CREDIT,
OR EXPERIENCE

IF YOU WANT TO BE A
REAL ESTATE INVESTOR
AND GET YOUR FIRST CHECK,
YOU NEED TO LEARN HOW TO
FLIP HOUSES AS A WHOLESALER
TO CASH BUYERS SO YOU CAN
EARN A $5,000 FINDER'S FEE

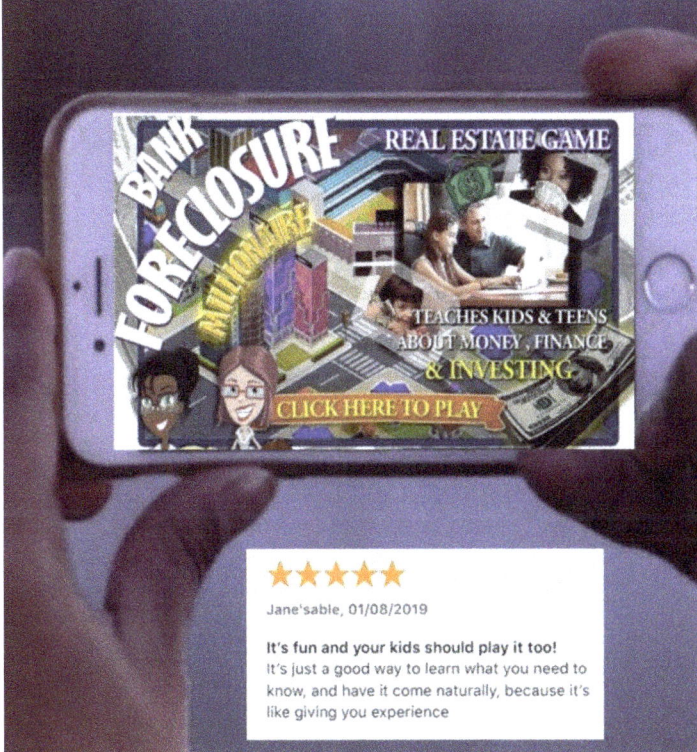

Click the link below or scan the QR code to view the video
https://www.youtube.com/watch?v=K1-_6iNVL_Y

Bank Foreclosure Millionaire
Is Now Famous!

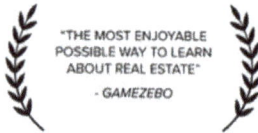

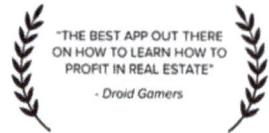

To read **AppAdvice** article click the link or scan QR code
https://appadvice.com//post/take-class-real-life-real-estate-investment-bank-foreclosure-millionaire/763434

To read **Gamezebo** article click the link or scan QR code
https://www.gamezebo.com/news/bank-foreclosure-millionaire-is-the-most-enjoyable-possible-way-to-learn-about-real-estate/

To read **DroidGamers** article click the link or scan QR code
https://www.droidgamers.com/news/bank-foreclosure-millionaire-is-a-fun-addictive-path-to-riches/

To learn about real estate with **Bank Foreclosure Millionaire** game click the link or scan the QR code
https://www.tapscape.com/bank-foreclosure-millionaire-game/

Purchase Details

You can purchase the full game or the full game with Terry Bontemps Mentoring & Coaching Program Included

Full Game

$19.99

Once you purchase the full game with

No Thanks

PURCHASE OPTIONS

PAYING $19.99 YOU GET ALL THESE LEVELS

The Most Intensive, Comprehensive, Educational 3-Day Training Course Ever Offered in the Real Estate Industry

1 WHOLESALING
I will teach you how to make $5,000 flipping houses to cash buyers

2 FIX & FLIP
I will teach you how to make 35,000 & 30% ROI rehabbing houses

3 LANDLORD
I will teach you how to build a rental portfolio making a 14% ROI 14% ROI

4 NOTE BUYING
I will teach you how to buy foreclosures directly from banks for 30%-50% below market value

5 MONEY PARTNERS
I will teach you how to get money from investors to fund your real estate deals

6 PRIVATE LENDERS
I will teach you how to get money from lenders so you can make more money

7 HARD MONEY LENDERS
I will teach you how to qualifying for loans without using your credit

8 HEDGE FUNDS
I will teach you how to buy bulk portfolios of notes & REOs from banks

9 AirBnB
I will teach you how to turn your home into a $5,200 a month cash flowing short term rental property

10 ASSISTED LIVING INVESTING
I will teach you how to turn ONE (1) house into $24,000 a month passive cash flow

Click the link below or scan QR code to download
Bank Foreclosure Millionaire from the Apple Store
https://apps.apple.com/us/app/bank-foreclosure-
millionaire/id1210462468

Click the link below or scan the QR code to download
Bank Foreclosure Millionaire from the Amazon Store
https://www.amazon.com/Bank-Foreclosure-Millionaire-
PROFITS-Flipping/dp/B07G2DMMVC

The houses on this page and the next page represent the blue houses that are in my Bank Foreclosure Millionaire game. These houses represent the gameplay for all levels except for level 4 and level 8. Players can click the blue houses in the game for level 1, 2, 3, 5, 6 & 7 to make money, build wealth, get rich and be real estate millionaires.

The foreclosure property which has a value of $150,000 and needs $20,000 of repairs is the case study. This is the property that the coach in the game uses as an example and it's also the numbers my student teaches you from in level 1, 2 and 3 training video.

DISTRESSED HOUSE BUYING
REAL ESTATE MARKET

FORECLOSURE

REO

HUD

CASE STUDY #1
After Repair Value: $150,000
Repairs Needed: $20,000
Asking: $89,000

Failed Business

ILLINOIS PROPERTY #1
After Repair Value: $250,000
Repairs Needed: $25,000
What's Your Exit Strategy?

Can't Afford Payments

CALIFORNIA PROPERTY #2
After Repair Value: $127,000
Repairs Needed: $17,500
What's Your Exit Strategy?

Tired of Being A Landlord

NEW YORK PROPERTY #2
After Repair Value: $375,000
Repairs Needed: $4,500
What's Your Exit Strategy?

CALIFORNIA PROPERTY #3
After Repair Value: $89,000
Repairs Needed: $3,000
What's Your Exit Strategy?

NEVADA PROPERTY #2
After Repair Value: $74,000
Repairs Needed: $6,500
What's Your Exit Strategy?

DISTRESSED HOUSE BUYING REAL ESTATE MARKET

For Sale By Owner

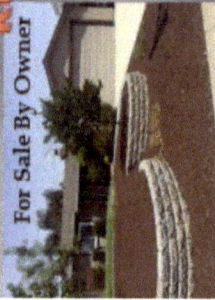

Owner Passed Away

Divorce

CALIFORNIA PROPERTY #1
After Repair Value: $77,000
Repairs Needed: $8,000
What's Your Exit Strategy?

NEVADA PROPERTY #1
After Repair Value: $109,000
Repairs Needed: $11,000
What's Your Exit Strategy?

ARIZONA PROPERTY #1
After Repair Value: $85,000
Repairs Needed: $9,500
What's Your Exit Strategy?

MLS

Bankruptcy

Probate

ILLINOIS PROPERTY #1
After Repair Value: $63,000
Repairs Needed: $6,000
What's Your Exit Strategy?

ARIZONA PROPERTY #2
After Repair Value: $97,000
Repairs Needed: $32,000
What's Your Exit Strategy?

NEW YORK #1
After Repair Value: $97,000
Repairs Needed: $32,000
What's Your Exit Strategy?

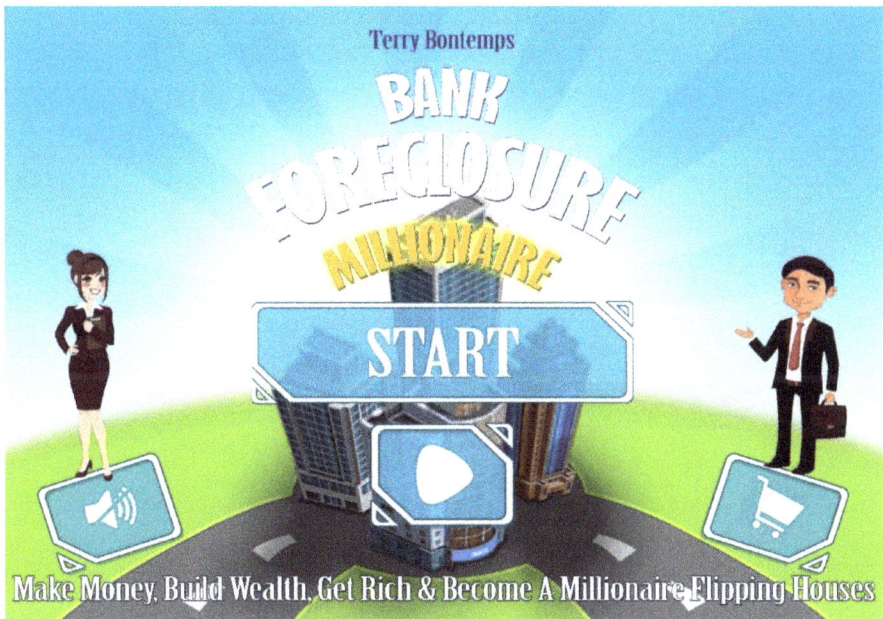

Terry Bontemps

BANK FORECLOSURE MILLIONAIRE

START

Make Money, Build Wealth, Get Rich & Become A Millionaire Flipping Houses

Game Play: The Different Assets in Bank Foreclosure Millionaire

To access any of the assets below simply tap the information icon, buildings, or symbols. This game is the culmination of forty-four years of actual real estate investing experience from the developer Terry Bontemps. He's invested in six states in the game including California, Arizona, Nevada, Illinois, New York and Florida.

1. **Built-in Coaching and Mentoring:** Tap the flashing "CLICK HERE FIRST" button on the main screen at every level of the game to get instructions on how to invest in real estate… Make Money, Build Wealth, GET RICH & Be A Millionaire. There are three ways for you to learn Terry's investment strategies. It's highly recommended you learn from all three. 1) Learn by listening to an audio 2) Learn by watching a video 3) Download the pdf to your phone.

2. **3D Virtual Game Board:** Game has $2.7 million dollars of real estate profits to earn. There are eight different levels of

187

gameplay. Game features real-life photos of houses that you can examine, purchase, and turn over for a nice profit. Some of the other features in the game include an award system, a live foreclosure auction, detailed video tutorials, investment case studies and more.

3. **Interactive Game Asks Financial Questions & Checks Your Answers Automatically For You:** There are over 345 questions making money as a real estate investor that you need to answer to complete the game. Answer the questions correctly and you receive a green checkmark. Answer the questions incorrectly, the game gives you a red checkmark which means the answer you gave was not correct. You must re-enter the correct answer to advance to the next level of the game.

4. **Financial Calculator:** There is a live calculator built into the game that allows players to input their answers and determine if they are correct or not when making offers on properties. It's located on the far-right hand side of the game where the flashing "i" is inside the circle.

5. **County Courthouse:** This represents the location where real estate documents are stored for record keeping like the deeds of trusts and mortgages. The county courthouse also represents the location where foreclosure auctions are held. It is an important aspect of the game as players can learn about the foreclosure process and how to buy properties at auction.

6. **The Bankruptcy Court**: This is where homeowners file bankruptcy whether it's chapter 7, 11 or 13. When a homeowner files bankruptcy it stops the foreclosure from happening on the county courthouse steps. This is called the "stay"

7. **Real Estate Office**: This is where the 11 blue houses are on the MLS. There are foreclosures, probate properties, bankruptcies, fire damaged properties, FSBO, etc.

8. **Digital Banking**: The digital bank is located on the right-hand side of the game. This is where the profits are stored when you make money and complete a real estate deal. Profits are automatically deposited into the digital bank. There's no need to go to the escrow company to pick up your cashier check.

9. **The Game Timer**: Is 60-minute timer located on the left-hand side of the game lets players learn investing skills quickly. Challenge yourself to beat your previous time or challenge friends and family to see who can make the most money in a set amount of time.

10. **Bank #1 & #2:** There are two banks represented in the game. These banks are involved in selling non-performing notes and foreclosed properties. Bank 2 has 174 first nonperforming loans they're interested in selling valued at $40 million. Bank 1 has 10 second nonperforming loans valued at $11 million that they're interested in selling.

11. **Commercial Building:** This represents a commercial property that a student of the game named Ron purchased from a bank. It showcases the potential for finding great note deals from banks that are nonperforming on commercial properties.

12. **Money Houses:** This represents the various nonperforming notes available in the game. Players can click on the money houses to see different notes with different amounts which could be first or second position liens. The money house in New York is the only note that has actual game play.

13. **Blue Houses:** These houses represent the gameplay for all levels except for level 4 and level 8. Players can click the blue houses in level 1, 2, 3, 5, 6 & 7 to make money in the game.

14. **Orange Houses**: These houses represent properties where the player has bought the note from the bank and modified the loan to allow the homeowner to keep their home.

Testimonial letters from homeowners are included.

15. **Rental Property:** This represents a rental property in the game. Players can click on it to learn about rental properties and how to earn a 14% return on investment.

16. **Hedge Fund Investor:** Click level 8 and follow the instructions of the coach in the game (audio). The bank has 174 nonperforming 1st loans valued at $40 million that you will flip to a hedge fund for a 1% finder fee. Level 8 only has one question for you to answer.

17. **Home Sweet Home:** This represents buying a home for you to own in the game. Players can click on it to learn about the process of buying a home.

18. **Airbnb Property**: This represents the potential for renting out your investment properties as Airbnb. Players can learn about the higher ROI and cash flow potential of owning short-term rentals compared to traditional rentals.

19. **Residential Assisted Living:** This represents the option of converting a property into a residential assisted living facility for the elderly. Players can learn about the potential income from housing elderly residents.

20. **Level Selection:** Click the start button on the game. You should see the LEVEL 1 screen on your smartphone. To select which level you want to play put the finger tip of your first finger on the wholesaler image. Hold your finger down on the screen inside the circle with the buildings and move the screen to the left. You should be able to navigate to any of the 8 levels.

21. **Level Selection Description:** Click the start button on the game. You should see the LEVEL 1 screen on your smartphone. To see a description of what each level will teach you. On the left side of the screen next to LEVEL 1, you should see this text "Please scroll up to see the real estate investment strategies used in the game to Make Money, Build

Wealth, Get Rich & Be A House Flipping Millionaire. Put the finger tip of your first finger on the top of this text. Hold your finger down on the screen. Move the screen upwards to see the descriptions.

22. **Button to Exit Out of Playing The Game:** In the bottom right hand corner of the game is a round circle with commercial buildings inside of it. Tap this button and it will take you back to the level selection screen. From this screen you can select any of the 8 levels you want to play.

These assets provide players with different scenarios and strategies to learn and practice various aspects of investing, making money, building wealth and becoming a real estate millionaire.

Enjoy!

Level - 1

Teach Me How To Get RICH
Wholesaling Houses

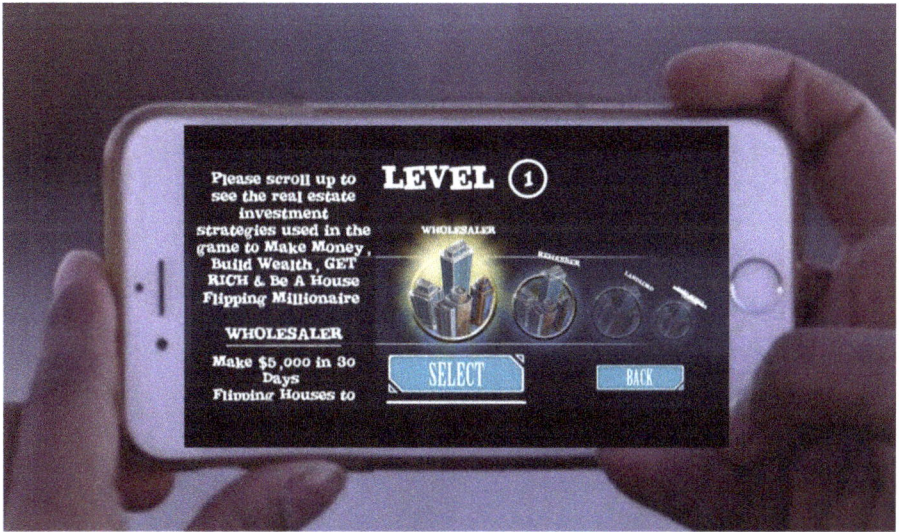

Please scroll up to see the real estate investment strategies used in the game to Make Money, Build Wealth, GET RICH & Be A House Flipping Millionaire

WHOLESALER

Make $5,000 in 30 Days Flipping Houses to

LEVEL ①

WHOLESALER
REHABBER
LANDLORD

SELECT   BACK

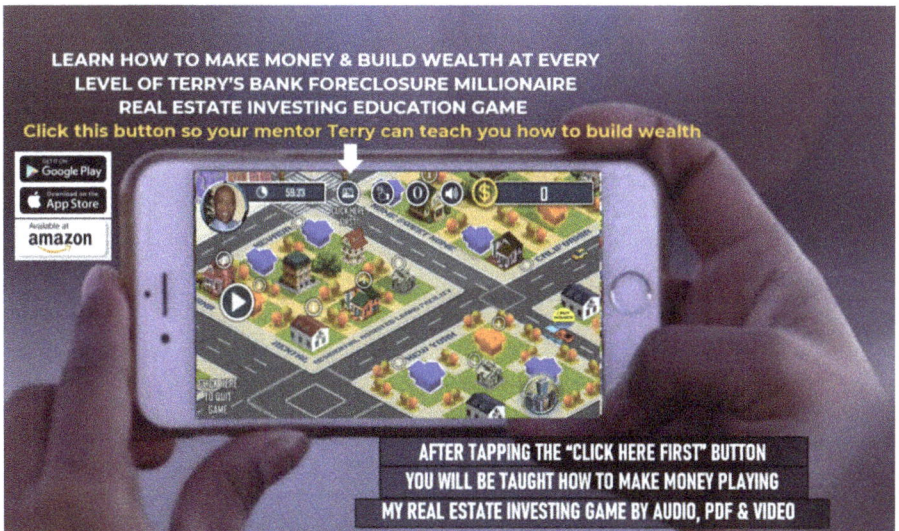

LEARN HOW TO MAKE MONEY & BUILD WEALTH AT EVERY LEVEL OF TERRY'S BANK FORECLOSURE MILLIONAIRE REAL ESTATE INVESTING EDUCATION GAME

Click this button so your mentor Terry can teach you how to build wealth

Google Play
App Store
Available at amazon

AFTER TAPPING THE "CLICK HERE FIRST" BUTTON YOU WILL BE TAUGHT HOW TO MAKE MONEY PLAYING MY REAL ESTATE INVESTING GAME BY AUDIO, PDF & VIDEO

Level 1 Real Estate Investor (Wholesaler) – Level 1 Real Estate Investor finds deals for other investors that have cash. A Level 1 Real Estate Investor makes his/her profit without having any money, credit, a job, or a real estate license. A) This investor's job is to find great deals and then flip them to an investor who has the money to close the transaction and receive a fee for finding the deal.

This investor likes to make $2,000 to $10,000 per transaction within 30 to 60 days. B) This investor can also find another investor to bring the money to close the deal, and they can split the profits. C) This investor can borrow the money to fund the deal from a private lender or hard money lender.

GET RICH FORMULA FOR FLIPPING HOUSES

Your Flip Fee for Level 1 is Always $5,000

ARV x 70% - Repairs = MAO (Maximum Allowable Offer)

ARV x 70% - Repairs - $5,000 For Your Fee = WMAO (Wholesale Maximum Allowable Offer)

WATCH ME DEMONSTRATE
MY BANK FORECLOSURE MILLIONAIRE
REAL ESTATE EDUCATION GAME

To view video, click the link or scan QR code below
https://www.youtube.com/watch?v=XwJo68gCwvk

YOU SUCCESSFULLY FLIPPED
11 HOUSES AS A WHOLESALER
IN LEVEL 1 OF MY GAME.
YOU'VE EARNED $55,000 IN PROFITS
AS A REAL ESTATE INVESTOR

HERE'S YOUR AWARD FOR BEING
A FINANCIALLY SUCCESSFUL
REAL ESTATE INVESTOR

GO AHEAD AND START LEVEL 2
FIX AND FLIP

MAKE SURE YOU LISTEN TO
THE COACH FOR INSTRUCTIONS

(TAP THE CLICK HERE FIRST BUTTON)

Congratulations!
You've graduated to the
Next Level of building wealth
& financial independence!

Level I-Wholesaler

Level - 2

Teach Me How To Get RICH

Rehabbing Houses

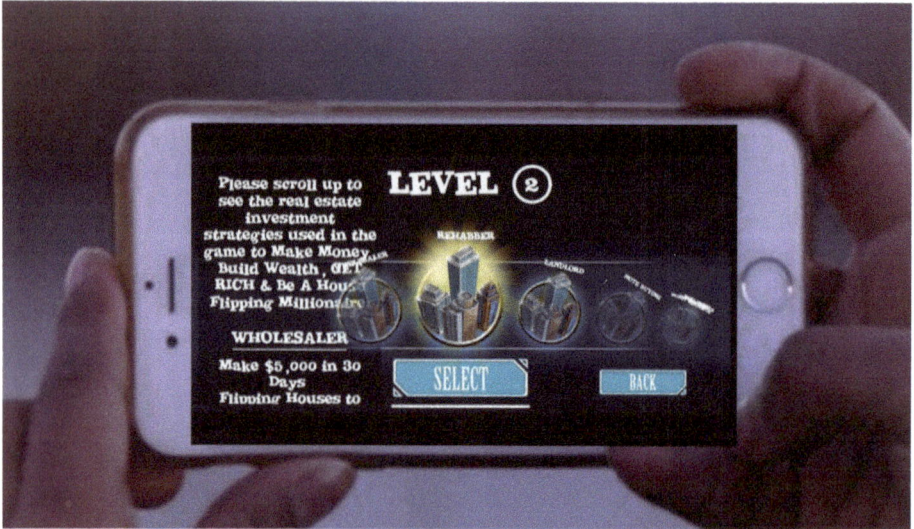

Please scroll up to see the real estate investment strategies used in the game to Make Money... Build Wealth , GET RICH & Be A House Flipping Millionaire

LEVEL ②

REHABBER

LANDLORD

WHOLESALER

Make $5,000 in 30 Days Flipping Houses to

SELECT

BACK

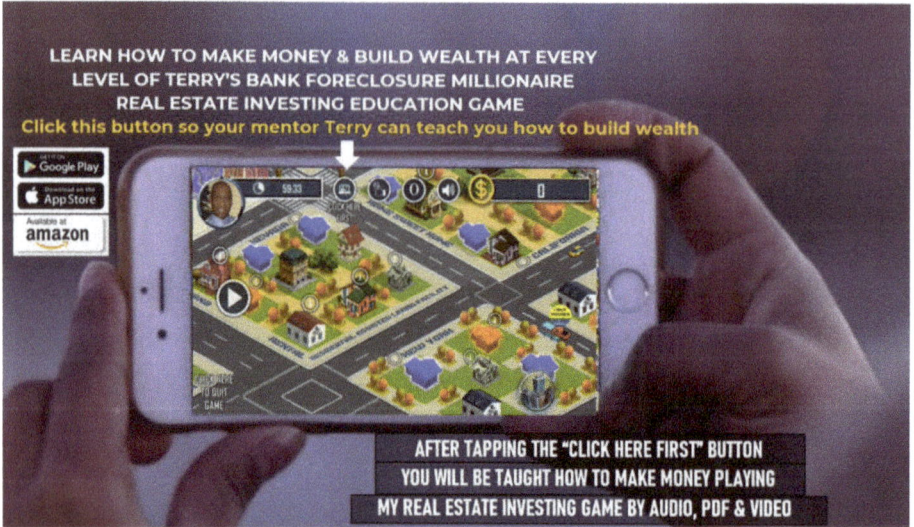

LEARN HOW TO MAKE MONEY & BUILD WEALTH AT EVERY LEVEL OF TERRY'S BANK FORECLOSURE MILLIONAIRE REAL ESTATE INVESTING EDUCATION GAME

Click this button so your mentor Terry can teach you how to build wealth

Google Play

App Store

Available at amazon

AFTER TAPPING THE "CLICK HERE FIRST" BUTTON YOU WILL BE TAUGHT HOW TO MAKE MONEY PLAYING MY REAL ESTATE INVESTING GAME BY AUDIO, PDF & VIDEO

Level 2 Real Estate Investor (Fix and Flipper) – A Level 2 Real Estate Investor makes his/her profit by rehabbing houses and selling them to first-time home buyers. This investor usually likes to make 20% of the fair market value of the property as a profit when he/she sells the house. A fix-and-flip investor likes to turn their money at least four times or more a year.

A Level 2 Real Estate Investor's job is to find the deal, manage it, rehab it, and sell it. Level 2 Real Estate Investors either have their own money, or they find a money partner or hard money lender to put up all the money to close the deal, including repairs, monthly payments, etc., for a share of the profit. A Level 2 Real Estate Investor must be able to find deals that can be purchased at the right price that produce a profit for him/her and the money partner. When you have the funds to make all-cash offers, you open doors to a nearly unlimited number of deals.

GET RICH FORMULA FOR REHABBING HOUSES

ARV x 70% - Repairs = MAO (maximum allowable offer)

ARV x 10% = COSTS

ARV x 20% = YOUR PROFIT

WATCH ME DEMONSTRATE MY BANK FORECLOSURE MILLIONAIRE REAL ESTATE EDUCATION GAME:

How to Make Your First Million Fixing & Flipping Houses
To view video, click the link, or scan the QR code below:
https://www.youtube.com/watch?v=EUp7x0qs5BA

YOU SUCCESSFULLY FIX AND FLIPPED
11 HOUSES AS A REHABBER
IN LEVEL 2 OF MY GAME

YOU'VE EARNED $287,600
AS A REAL ESTATE INVESTOR

HERE'S YOUR AWARD FOR
BEING A FINANCIALLY SUCCESSFUL
REAL ESTATE INVESTOR

GO AHEAD AND START
LEVEL 3 LANDLORD

MAKE SURE YOU LISTEN TO
THE COACH FOR INSTRUCTIONS

(TAP THE CLICK HERE FIRST BUTTON)

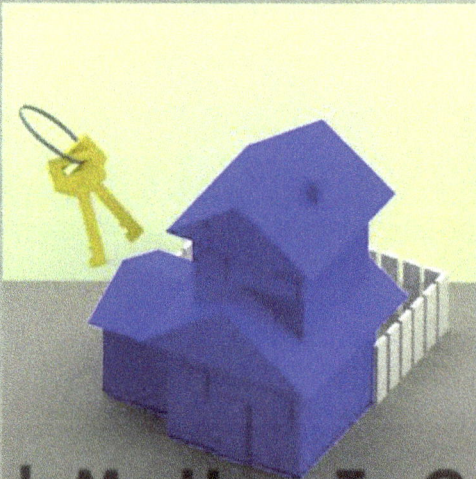

Level - 3

Teach Me How To Get
Building A Rental Portfolio

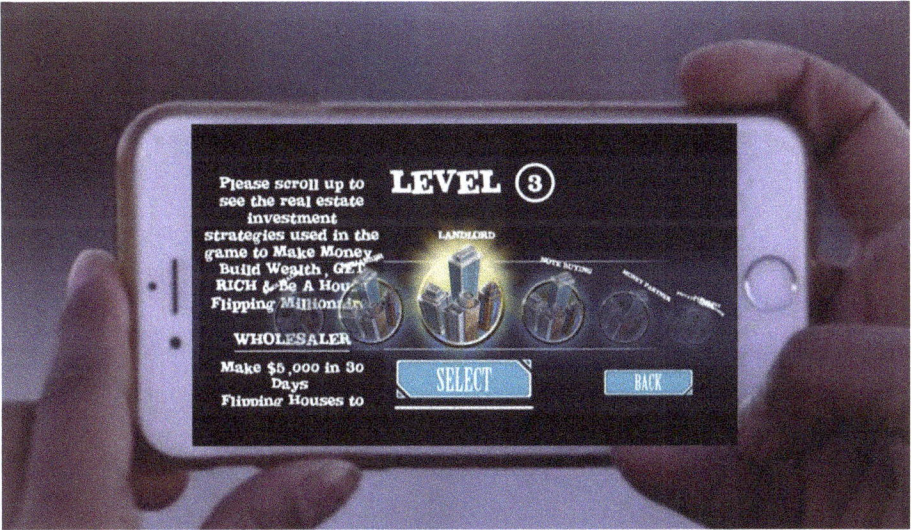

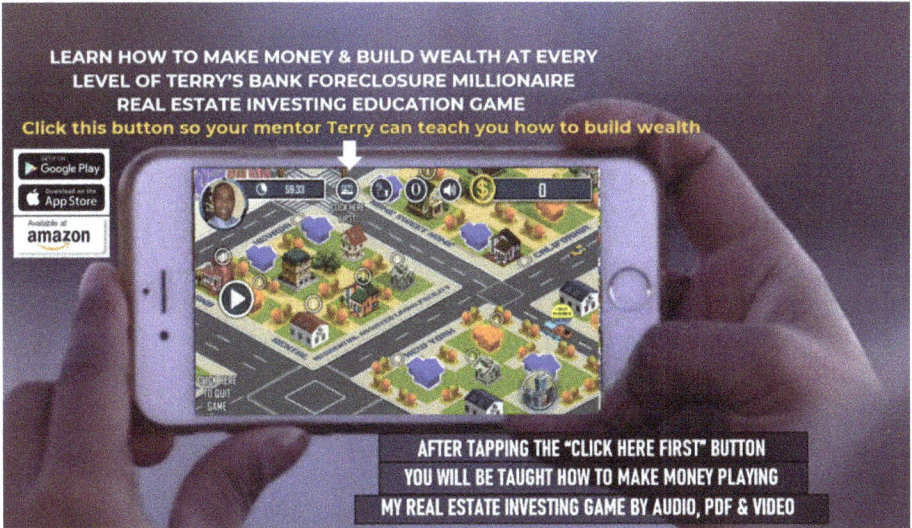

LEARN HOW TO MAKE MONEY & BUILD WEALTH AT EVERY
LEVEL OF TERRY'S BANK FORECLOSURE MILLIONAIRE
REAL ESTATE INVESTING EDUCATION GAME

Click this button so your mentor Terry can teach you how to build wealth

AFTER TAPPING THE "CLICK HERE FIRST" BUTTON
YOU WILL BE TAUGHT HOW TO MAKE MONEY PLAYING
MY REAL ESTATE INVESTING GAME BY AUDIO, PDF & VIDEO

Level 3 Real Estate Investor (Landlord) – A Level 3 Real Estate Investor makes his/her profit by renting property to tenants, which is a way to build and retain wealth. The landlord wants passive income, which is income that comes in regardless of whether they're working or not.

A Level 3 Real Estate Investor invests for cash flow each and every month. This investor likes to make a 12% or better return on his/her investment (ROI). Level 3 Real Estate Investors like long-term profits.

GET RICH FORMULA FOR BEING A LANDLORD

MAO + Repairs + Costs = Investment

Investment x 14% Divided by 12 = Rental Payment

Investment Divided by Rent = Months to Get Investment

WATCH ME DEMONSTRATE MY
BANK FORECLOSURE MILLIONAIRE
REAL ESTATE EDUCATION GAME:

How to Make Your First Million Building
A Rental Portfolio As A Landlord

To view video click the link, or scan QR code below
https://www.youtube.com/watch?v=I7cKRdpJzbM

YOU SUCCESSFULLY RENTED 11
HOUSES AS A LANDLORD IN LEVEL 3
OF MY GAME. YOU'VE EARNED
$141,804 A YEAR OF PASSIVE INCOME
AS A REAL ESTATE INVESTOR

HERE'S YOUR AWARD FOR BEING
A FINANCIALLY SUCCESSFUL
REAL ESTATE INVESTOR

GO AHEAD AND START LEVEL 4
NOTE-BUYING. GO TO
THE NEW YORK PROPERTY

CLICK THE MONEY HOUSE
TO PLAY THE GAME

MAKE SURE YOU LISTEN TO THE
COACH FOR INSTRUCTIONS

(TAP THE CLICK HERE FIRST BUTTON)

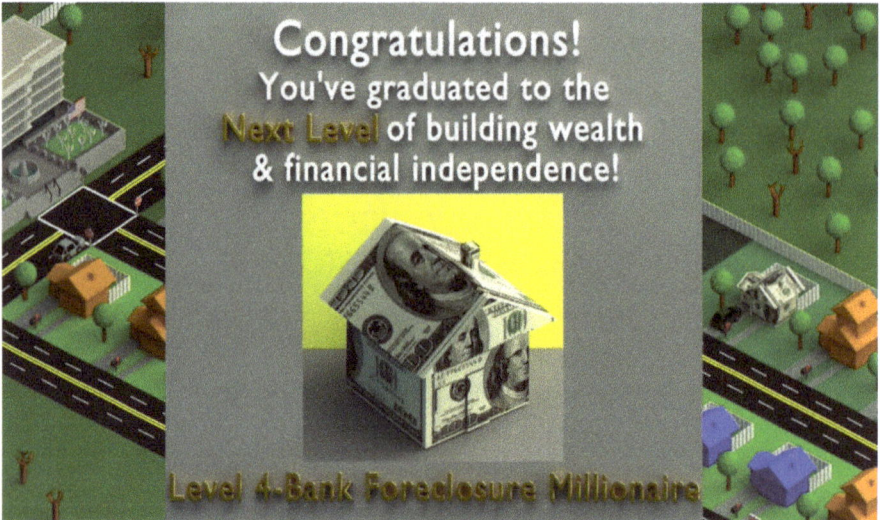

Congratulations!
You've graduated to the
Next Level of building wealth
& financial independence!

Level 4-Bank Foreclosure Millionaire

IN ORDER FOR YOU TO
PLAY LEVEL 4 THROUGH LEVEL 8,
YOU MUST PAY $19.99 FOR MY
REAL ESTATE INVESTING GAME

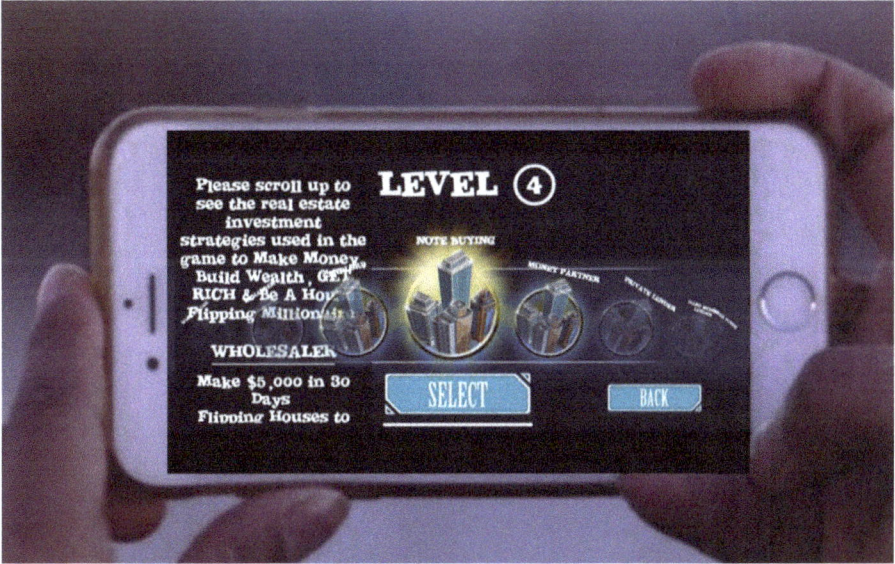

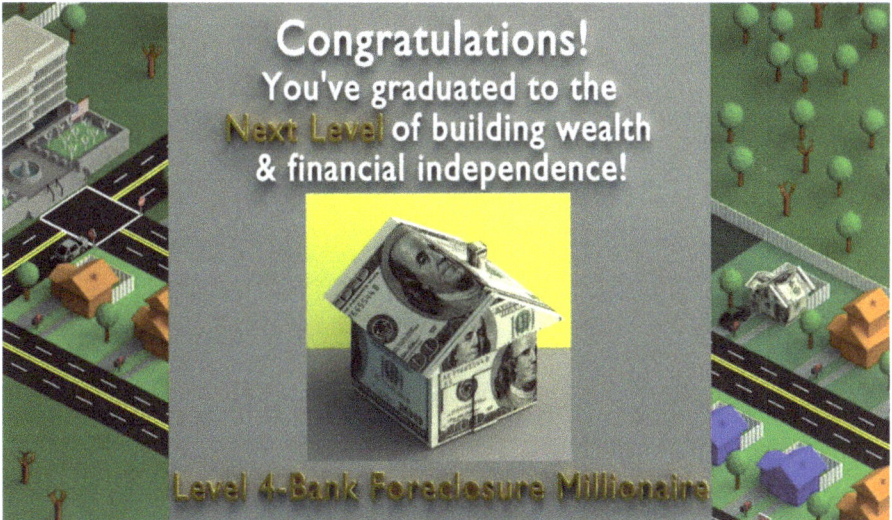

Congratulations!
You've graduated to the
Next Level of building wealth
& financial independence!

Level 4-Bank Foreclosure Millionaire

WATCH ME DEMONSTRATE
MY BANK FORECLOSURE
MILLIONAIRE REAL ESTATE
EDUCATION GAME:

How to Make Your First Million

Buying Notes From Banks Below Market Value
To view video, click the link or scan QR code below:
https://www.youtube.com/watch?v=mYq4TYsE92s

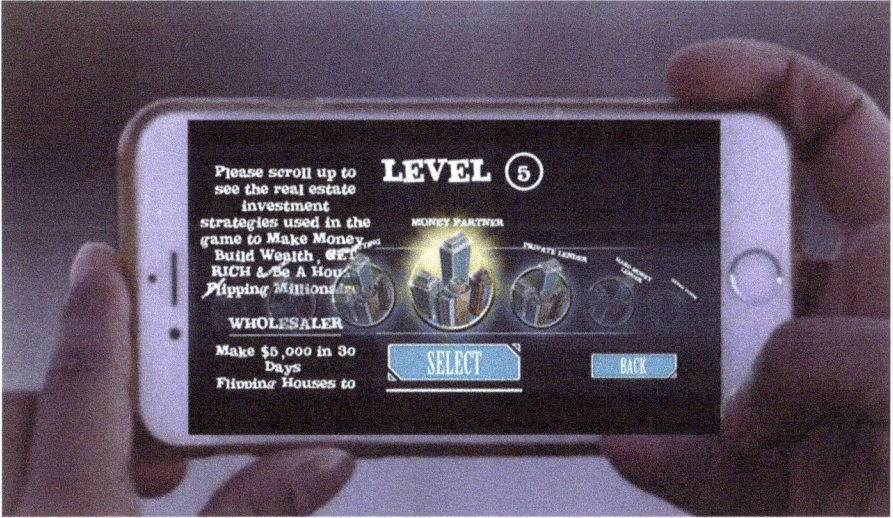

Please scroll up to see the real estate investment strategies used in the game to Make Money, Build Wealth, GET RICH & Be A House Flipping Millionaire

LEVEL ⑤

MONEY PARTNER

PRIVATE LENDER

HARD MONEY LENDER

WHOLESALER

Make $5,000 in 30 Days Flipping Houses to

SELECT   BACK

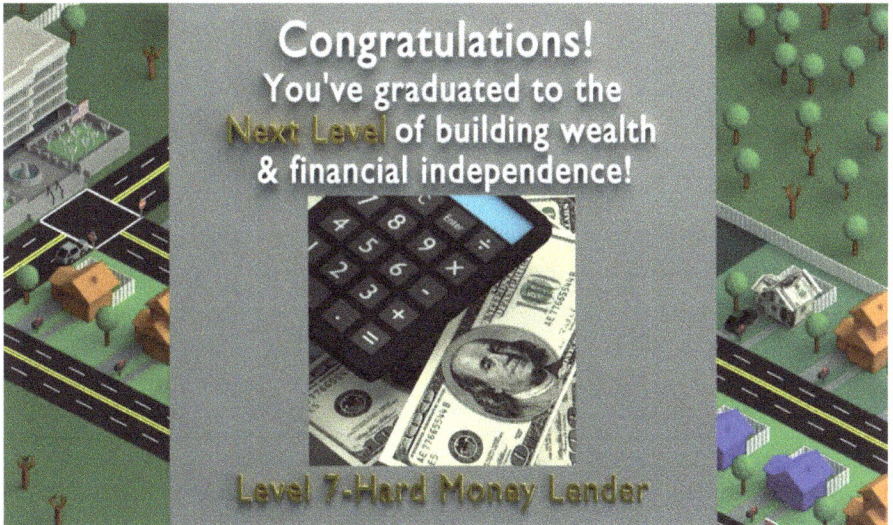

Congratulations!
You've graduated to the
Next Level of building wealth
& financial independence!

Level 7-Hard Money Lender

WATCH ME DEMONSTRATE
MY BANK FORECLOSURE
MILLIONAIRE REAL ESTATE
EDUCATION GAME:

How to Make Your First Million Borrowing
Money From Money Partners

To view video, click the link or scan QR code below:
https://www.youtube.com/watch?v=Cl1LaQr6M9s

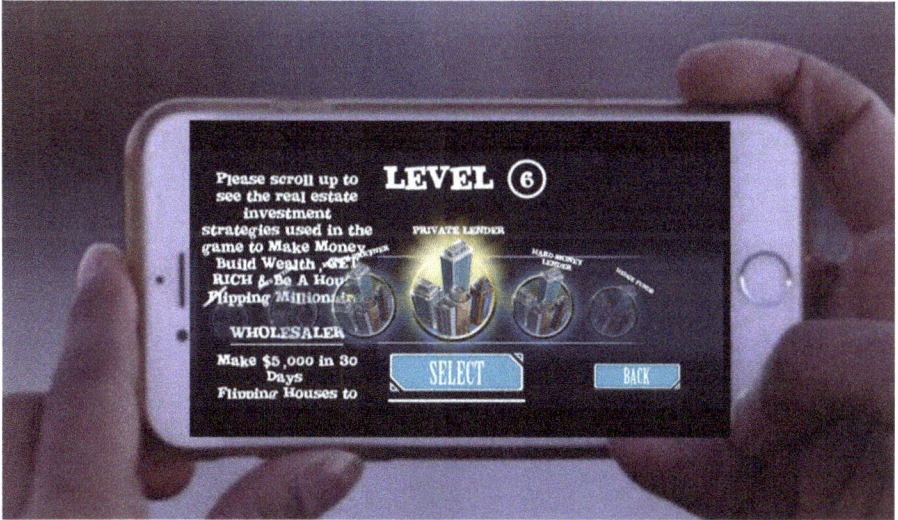

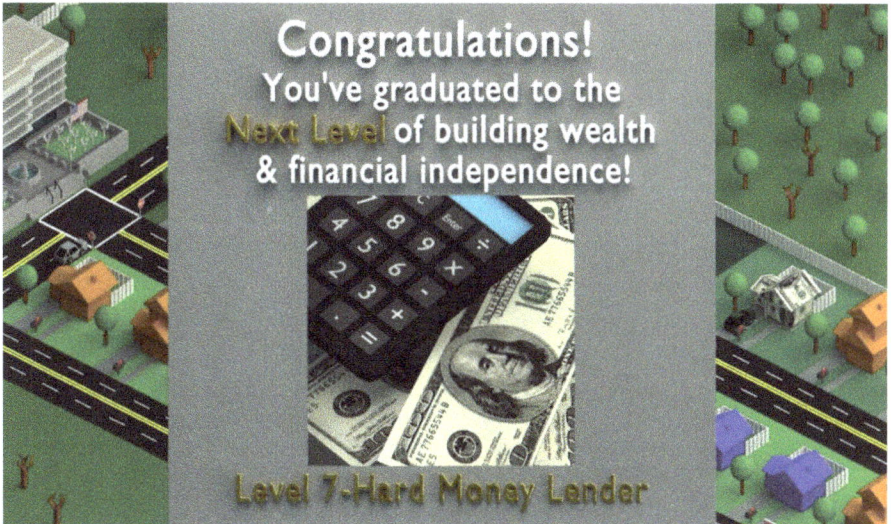

Congratulations!
You've graduated to the
Next Level of building wealth
& financial independence!

Level 7-Hard Money Lender

WATCH ME DEMONSTRATE MY BANK FORECLOSURE MILLIONAIRE REAL ESTATE EDUCATION GAME:

How to Make Your First Million
Borrowing Money From Private Lenders

To view video, click the link or scan QR code below:
https://www.youtube.com/watch?v=mj79WWNrh0k

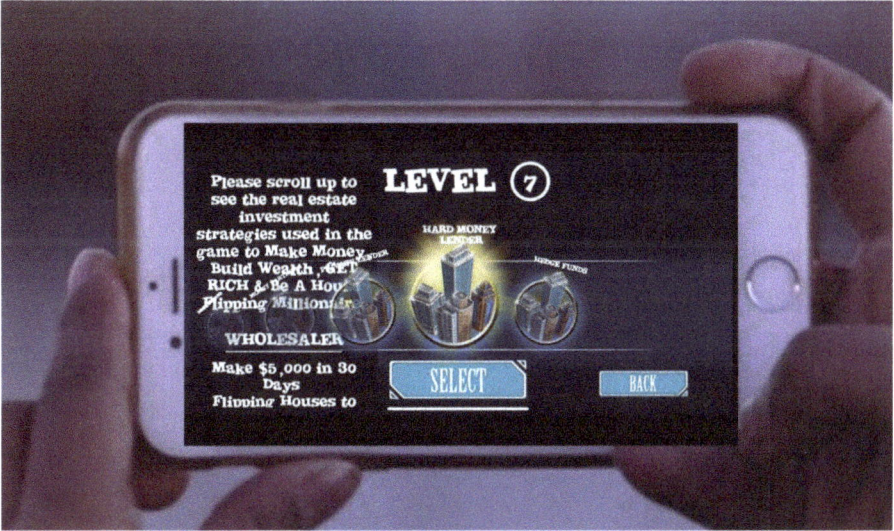

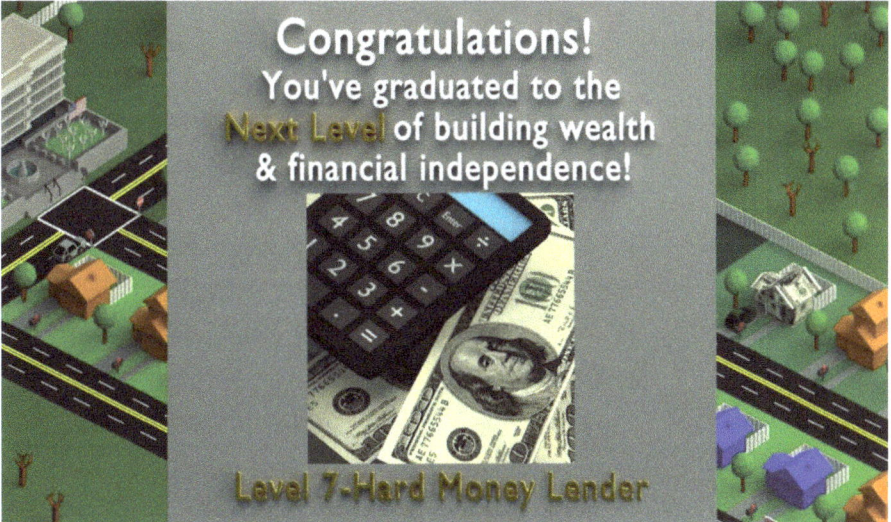

Congratulations!
You've graduated to the
Next Level of building wealth
& financial independence!

Level 7-Hard Money Lender

WATCH ME DEMONSTRATE MY BANK FORECLOSURE MILLIONAIRE REAL ESTATE EDUCATION GAME:

How to Make Your First Million
Borrowing Money From Hard Money Lenders

To view video, click the link or scan QR code below:
https://www.youtube.com/watch?v=CREbbVCNTZI

Please scroll up to see the real estate investment strategies used in the game to Make Money, Build Wealth, GET RICH & Be A House Flipping Millionaire

LEVEL 8

HEDGE FUNDS

WHOLESALER

Make $5,000 in 30 Days Flipping Houses to

SELECT   BACK

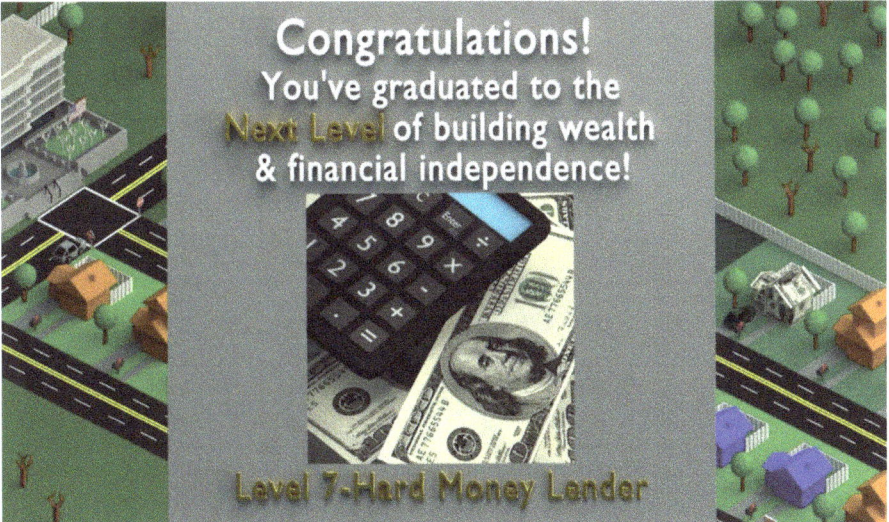

Congratulations!
You've graduated to the
Next Level of building wealth
& financial independence!

Level 7-Hard Money Lender

WATCH ME DEMONSTRATE
MY BANK FORECLOSURE
MILLIONAIRE REAL ESTATE
EDUCATION GAME:

How to Make Your First Million Flipping
Notes and REO's to Hedge Funds

To view video, click the link or scan QR code below:
https://www.youtube.com/watch?v=NRLwpgT1LMM

216

BANK FORECLOSURE MILLIONAIRE
BIG PROFITS HOUSE FLIPPING GAME

WATCH THE 4 MINUTE MOVIE HERE

To view movie, click the link or scan QR code below:
https://www.youtube.com/watch?v=Ynvgg3-bauo

"Bank Foreclosure Millionaire" Can Help Parents Teach Their Children Finances, Financial Literacy and Investing

Bank Foreclosure Millionaire is an educational real estate investing game that can be a valuable tool for parents to teach their children about finances, financial literacy, and investing. Here is an extensive presentation on how Bank Foreclosure Millionaire can help parents in this regard:

1. **Introduction:**
   - Bank Foreclosure Millionaire is an addictive house flipping real estate investment game that simulates the real-world experience of buying, selling, renting, and flipping houses.
   - It is a fun, challenging, and educational game that teaches players how to make money investing in real estate.
   - By playing this game, children can learn important financial concepts and skills that will benefit them in the future.

2. **Financial Literacy:**
   - Bank Foreclosure Millionaire teaches children about the basics of financial literacy, such as budgeting, saving, and investing.
   - Players learn how to evaluate and structure real estate deals, analyze the numbers, and make informed financial decisions.
   - They also learn about different investment strategies, how to raise money for real estate deals, and how to manage their finances effectively.

3. **Real-World Experience:**
   - The game provides a realistic simulation of the real estate market, allowing children to experience the challenges

and opportunities of real estate investing.

- They learn about market trends, property valuation, negotiation skills, and the importance of timing in real estate transactions.
- This real-world experience helps children develop critical thinking, problem-solving, and decision-making skills.

4. **Wealth Building:**

- Bank Foreclosure Millionaire emphasizes the importance of building wealth through real estate investing.
- Children learn how to make profitable investment decisions, generate passive income through rental properties, and build a real estate portfolio.
- They also learn about the long-term benefits of investing, such as financial independence, retirement planning, and creating generational wealth.

5. **Entrepreneurship:**

- The game encourages children to think like entrepreneurs and develop a business mindset.
- They learn about finding deals, managing renovations, marketing properties, and maximizing profits.
- This entrepreneurial mindset fosters creativity, innovation, and a proactive approach to financial success.

6. **Parental Involvement:**

- Bank Foreclosure Millionaire provides an opportunity for parents to actively engage with their children in learning about finances and investing.
- Parents can play the game with their children, guide them through the decision- making process, and discuss the financial concepts and strategies involved.
- This hands-on involvement strengthens the parent-child bond and creates a supportive learning environment.

7. **Practical Application:**

- The knowledge and skills gained from playing Bank Foreclosure Millionaire can be applied in real life.

- Children can use the principles they learn to make informed financial decisions, invest in real estate, and build wealth in the future.

- This practical application of knowledge helps children develop financial independence and prepares them for a successful financial future.

Conclusion: Bank Foreclosure Millionaire is an invaluable tool for parents to teach their children about finances, financial literacy, and investing. By playing this game, children can gain practical knowledge, develop important financial skills, and cultivate a mindset for financial success. It provides a fun and interactive way to learn about real estate investing and prepares children for a financially secure future.

We All Want to Be Wealthy. You want to be wealthy. Your mother wants to be wealthy. Your uncle wants to be wealthy, too.

We all have dreams and aspirations of being wealthy, but if you don't have a plan or a strategy, you have very little chance of being wealthy.

—Terry Bontemps

Chapter 9 Takeaways and Actionable Steps For You To Take

Chapter 9: Discusses a mobile app called "Bank Foreclosure Millionaire" that serves as an educational real estate investing game. The chapter highlights the features and benefits of the game, as well as the skills and knowledge that players can gain from playing it. Here are the key takeaways and actionable items from this chapter:

1. The game is designed to teach players about real estate investing and wealth-building strategies. It simulates the experience of buying, selling, renting, and flipping houses, allowing players to learn about market trends, property valuation, negotiation skills, and timing in real estate transactions.

2. The game is suitable for anyone, regardless of their financial situation or experience. It is specifically targeted towards those who have been locked out of the wealth- building experience due to lack of money, credit, or previous investing experience.

3. The game is divided into different levels, each representing a different type of real estate investor. Level 1 focuses on wholesaling, where players find deals and flip them to cash buyers for a fee. Level 2 focuses on fix and flipping, where players rehab houses and sell them for a profit. Level 3 focuses on becoming a landlord and generating passive income through rental properties. Level 4 is note buying. Level 5 is about finding a money partner to fund your real estate deals. Level 6 is finding a private lender to fund your deals. Level 7 is finding a hard money lender. Level 8 is working with hedge funds and bulk REOs.

4. The game provides formulas and strategies for each level, such as calculating maximum allowable offers, determining repair costs, and setting profit margins. These formulas can be applied in real-life investing scenarios.

5. The game encourages players to think like entrepreneurs and develop a business mindset. It teaches them how to find deals, manage renovations, market properties, and maximize profits.

6. The game can be played individually or with the guidance of a mentor or coach. It provides a hands-on learning experience and allows players to apply their knowledge in real-life investment scenarios.

7. The game emphasizes the importance of financial literacy, budgeting, saving, and investing. It teaches players how to make informed financial decisions, generate passive income, and build long-term wealth.

8. The complete game with all levels open with endless game play can be downloaded from the Amazon or Apple Store for $19.99.

Overall, the chapter highlights the benefits of using the Bank Foreclosure Millionaire game as a tool for learning about real estate investing and wealth-building. It provides actionable items for players to apply their knowledge and skills in real-life investment scenarios, ultimately helping them achieve financial freedom and build generational wealth.

INTERVIEW WITH AUTHOR TERRY BONTEMPS, CONDUCTED BY DONNA KOZIK

Wealth teacher, thought leader, and bank note-buying expert Terry Bontemps discusses with me his new book, *Wealth For The Rest Of Us*, how anyone NOT WEALTHY can acquire wealth, own a home, and invest in real estate regardless of their credit score and what they have or don't have in their bank account.

Too many people have been locked out of the wealth-building game – until now. It's time for you to achieve true financial freedom (in your lifetime) and change the trajectory of your family finances forever.

Wealth For The Rest Of Us levels the playing field. My book is a practical, step-by-step guide to how anyone can acquire wealth, multiply their wealth, keep wealth, and be able to pass generational wealth down to family members.

For centuries, wealth in America has been reserved for and accessible by a chosen few. But for the rest of us, wealth remains an unattainable goal and a game that many have never been allowed to play.

In this book, Terry Bontemps – wealth teacher, thought leader and bank note buying expert – shares the strategies he's used to build his own real estate empire and to coach his students through their own journeys to multiple-million-dollar real estate investment portfolios.

While most real estate millionaires remain silent about how they really made their money, Terry teaches you exactly how the big deals are done.

As it stands right now, we really haven't seen another thought leader and teacher who has come up in the space around creating wealth in quite some time.

There was Suze Orman, there was Robert Kiyosaki, and there have been a couple of other ones that kind of played around in that space but never really took on the mantra. Terry Bontemps is uniquely positioned as a thought leader in the wealth development space.

Does Robert Kiyosaki deal in the real estate space? Yes! Does Terry Bontemps deal in the real estate space? Yes!

Does Robert Kiyosaki have a game? Yes, it's called "Cash Flow." Does Terry Bontemps have a game? Yes, it's called "Bank Foreclosure Millionaire."

Does Robert Kiyosaki have a book? Yes, it's called *Rich Dad-Poor Dad*. Does Terry Bontemps have a book? Yes, it's called *Wealth For The Rest Of Us*.

Does Robert Kiyosaki deal in the wealth development space? Yes!

Does Terry Bontemps deal in the wealth development space? Yes!

Welcome, Terry!

Where are you in the world?

> Sacramento, California

What is that area most known for?

> Being the capital of California. It's known for being both the "city of trees" and the "farm to fork" capitol. Sacramento is known for historical sites, such as the State Capitol, Capitol Park, Old Town, Sutter's Fort, and the Railroad Museum.

How do you start your day on the right foot? What is your business passion?

> Rising at 6 a.m. for studying, writing, and going for a 2 ½ mile walk with my wife and her friends. The coldest morning for our walk was 34 degrees, but we did it. My mission, ministry, and passion for the last 23 years has been teaching everyday regular people how to acquire wealth, keep wealth, multiply their wealth, and pass wealth down to their family by investing in real estate. I do this through my highly interactive coaching, mentoring, software, and real estate training programs.

Tell me about yourself related to what you do as a coach.

> My name is Terry Bontemps. I'm a wealth teacher, thought leader, and bank note buying expert.

> I'm the number one bank foreclosure mentor in the United States. I bought my first home in 1980 when I was 20 years old. If there is

one thing that I've known my whole life, it is that I would ultimately never work for anyone.

Why are you writing about this topic?

Because 78% of the people in the United States are living paycheck-to-paycheck. Because of this, so many people have been and are being locked out of the wealth-building experience.

Who, specifically are you hoping to reach with this message?

Wealth For The Rest of Us is my wealth plan that takes everyday people, which includes the middle class, minorities, marginalized communities, and the poor who are not bankable to wealth from where they're at currently in life!

What are some common challenges or situations people struggling with this topic face?

What the experts won't and don't tell you about wealth is that oftentimes, many of the wealth-building strategies out there won't work for the majority of minorities, marginalized communities, people in the middle class, and poor.

1. Traditional wealth-building strategies were developed mainly for people who were already wealthy.

2. The traditional criteria and requirements for anyone interested in building wealth is that they need to have money in the bank, good credit, and previous investing experience (example: accredited investor).

3. The real estate and banking industries perpetuate the myth that people who don't have credit, capital, experience, or credentials can't buy a home for their family or invest in real estate.

How can they get started in overcoming these challenges?

First of all, there are way too many people who believe that you need money, credit, and experience to buy a home, and start INVESTING in real estate, and it's simply NOT TRUE!

When the truth is, what you need to have is the know-how. The truth is what you need to have is the savvy. The truth is what you need to have is the strategy. The truth is you need to have the relationship.

And, so, for many of us, we're missing the strategy. We're missing the savvy, we're missing the mentoring, we're missing the consistency, and we're missing the know-how.

So many deserving people have been locked out of the WEALTH-BUILDING EXPERIENCE due to what they didn't know or what they believed to be true. That all changes today!

Share a story about yourself related to this topic and how you became interested in it and how it relates to the topic of building wealth.

I have the back story of how important real estate is to building wealth, and what it's done for me and my family. It's how I've been able to create generational wealth, leave a legacy, and an inheritance to my children.

Describe a challenge in life you've overcome. What was it and how did you overcome it?

I lost two houses to foreclosure. I lost $25,000 on one real estate deal and $25,000 on another, so I know what it's like to be in the struggle financially. I also know what it takes to overcome life's challenges and be victorious.

One of the lowest points of my life was when I had to go live with my daughter after losing my house to foreclosure. Even though I was down emotionally, physically, financially, and spiritually, I didn't want to let my family down.

Somehow, I found the energy to get back out there, and I figured out how to make money in real estate with bad credit and very little money.

What would people be surprised to find out about you?

I've been helping homeowners all across the United States keep their homes, and making money as a real estate investor buying notes directly from banks. I've helped homeowners in Florida, New York, California, Nevada, Illinois, and Arizona keep their homes instead of losing them to investors or the foreclosure auction.

One person I helped to keep his home was guy named Earl. Earl lived in Las Vegas. He was a military veteran. Earl's primary concern was not losing his VA loan because that's how he bought his home. If he had lost his VA loan, he would never be able to use the VA to buy another home.

Earl was recently divorced, dealing with family law court and the IRS. He had an unreliable automobile to get him to work, and his house needed $4,400 in repairs.

He had no equity in his home, and he couldn't pay a real estate agent to sell his home. The only thing I could see happening to his home was it going to foreclosure.

He was $42,000 behind on his first mortgage, and $6,000 behind on his second. I didn't know when I bought his note that he was $42,000 behind on his payments. It was a big surprise to me. I paid the $42,000 to bring his loan current.

I spent $4,400 of my own money to repair his home. Earl was able to "keep his home." Earl told me he could make his payments.

Earl didn't make his payments. He fell behind $18,000 on his first loan. I had to pay the $18,000 so I wouldn't lose the $46,000 I previously invested in Earl's home.

At this point, I told Earl that he couldn't really afford his house and that if he didn't sell it, he would end up losing it to foreclosure and lose his VA loan. He agreed, and he wrote me a testimonial letter thanking me for helping him keep his home.

Outside of your family, what is one of your proudest accomplishments?

I recently remodeled a rental property that I've owned since 1999. I had originally planned to sell it because the real estate market was hot. By the time I finished the remodel, the market dropped, and interest rates increased. I had three different buyers back out of buying it. I decided to rent it to two women who had previously been homeless.

One lady was 63. She was a grandmother who had raised her two grandchildren for 10 years. She was living in motels and in her vehicle for the previous two years before I met her.

She now has a clean, affordable, safe, and newly remodeled home to live in. The bathroom and kitchen are brand new, with a new stove, refrigerator, tub, shower, and cabinets. I feel very proud of being able to provide homes to both women.

What's on your upside down bucket list? (What have you already done that you're so happy you did?)

#1 — I'm so happy I decided to get out of debt. I have no debt on my home or rental properties. I have no credit card debt, automobile debt, or student loan debt, and I don't owe banks any money.

#2 — I'm at the point I don't have to work for money anymore. I don't have to do another real estate deal in my life. It's because I have no debt and monthly cash flow from my rentals.

#3 — I'm able to leave an inheritance to my children, because I've set up a revocable living trust. The trust is a private document that avoids probate. The trust designates where the assets will go.

Pick four sentences that describe you.

1. Indomitable spirit
2. Determined
3. Never gives up
4. Finishes what I start

List your favorite books or movies.

1. *The Banker*
2. *The Pursuit of Happiness*
3. *My 5-Day "Build Your Wealth" Challenge*

Favorite dessert?

German Chocolate Cake

*The Goal of Every Man and Woman
Should Be Financial Freedom.*

Be That Wealthy Person!

*REAL CONVERSATIONS WE SHOULD BE HAVING
IN OUR COMMUNITY ABOUT BUILDING WEALTH.*

—Terry Bontemps

Learn how to make money, build wealth, and be a real estate millionaire. Teach your kids and teens about money, finance, and investing. Download Terry's mobile app Bank Foreclosure Millionaire from Amazon or Apple Store today, $19.99.

TERRY BONTEMPS

FROM BEGGING THE BANK TO BECOMING THE BANK

Meet the Man Who Is Making More Investors Bank Foreclosure Millionaires By Owning Bank Notes

A powerhouse in the world of finance, investing, real estate, and wealth building, Terry Bontemps' teachings are unconventional. His results are irrefutable. And his impact? Undeniable.

When someone says their mentor taught them how to turn $110,000 into $1.2 million and a 1090% return on their investment, you immediately want to know who they learned from. Fortunately, the world now knows his name, and it's Terry Bontemps.

A legendary businessman, real estate investor, millionaire mentor, and financial software developer, Terry is an industry-leading authority on bank note buying and buying foreclosures from banks. His unprecedented methodology teaches people how to build lasting wealth through real estate and multiply money faster than any other investment vehicle. A razor-sharp strategist, Terry began buying the financial instruments called "bank notes" in 2001, and hasn't looked back.

While other so-called real estate investment gurus are selling the outdated, big-risk-little-reward rehabbing approach as the sole key to success, Terry shifts his students' sights from becoming real estate flippers and landlords to "being bankers" by owning the real estate financing.

Singlehandedly rewriting the wealth code rules and legacies for real estate investors worldwide, Terry is redefining the face of the modern millionaire, eliminating credit, previous investing experience, and capital as the traditional criteria for wealth building. Using his rarely-taught-before investment strategy of "being the bank", Terry has the keys to unlock billions of dollars of profits that traditionally were only available primarily to other financial institutions, insurance companies, ultra-wealth individuals, and trusts. Accelerating asset and wealth accumulation by the millions, Terry takes everyday people from counted out to counting cash – and lots of it.

When he asked his uncle, who was a real estate investor, how he'd become rich his uncle gave him some simple, yet sage, wisdom that would change his life, and that was to save his money, buy a house, and pay it off. Taking those instructions to heart, Terry did exactly that.

232

HE
WHO
OWNS
HIMSELF

I f there is one thing that Terry Bontemps has known all his life, it's that he would ultimately never work for anyone.

Born to forge his own path to financial freedom—and lead others to theirs—he is an entrepreneur at his core. And he knew that he was destined to not be beholden to anything, especially a job, bank, or conventional thinking.

Without yet knowing how he'd make that his reality, he started his first business selling ten cords of firewood on the corner in the neighborhood where he lived. Today, it's been thirty years since he's punched a clock for a paycheck, asked a bank for a loan, used his credit, or borrowed any money to purchase the real estate he currently owns.

He is a man who holds complete control over his cash flow, his life, and his legacy. A man who dictates his own financial success. A man who moves with a fearlessness who has amassed his fortune investing in real estate by "Being The Bank."

A MOGUL IN THE MAKING

At twenty years old, Terry had what he now knows was a destiny-defining conversation.

With an inexplicable desire to make his money, and lots of it, he turned to the only person he knew who would teach him the way, and that was his uncle.

When he asked him how he'd become rich, that uncle, who was a real estate investor, gave him some simple, yet sage, wisdom that would change his life, and that was to save his money, buy a house, and pay it off. Taking those instructions to heart, Terry did exactly that.

From that conversation, he embarked on a 40+ year, and still counting, career in real estate buying foreclosure properties directly from banks. The moves he made in the early were fearless but far from flawless. He lost two of his own homes to foreclosure but bounced back every time with nothing but vengeance and a renewed fire to secure his family's legacy and other families' too. Terry buys notes from banks with the sole purpose of helping homeowners facing foreclosure keep their homes instead of losing them at the courthouse steps to investors. His profit meets public service approach creates a win-win-win solution for him, the banks, and the homeowners.

Today, he's invested in bank notes in six different real estate markets including California, Arizona, Nevada, Illinois, Florida, and New York.

BECOMING THE
BANK OF BONTEMPS

Terry began relentlessly studying money, wealth building, investing, and real estate. While he's invested $200K + to elevate his expertise, back then, his brazenness alone bought him into the right rooms. Terry learned early that exposure, education, and conversations are capital. He soon realized that the fix-and-flip route his industry heralded as the holy grail of investing was a trickle of coins compared to the multiplication of money available through acquiring bank notes.

What Terry didn't have in capital, he made up for in courage. Taking a risk that few rookies have the heart for, he set out to broker a deal between a hedge fund and a bank that was selling a portfolio of 174 notes worth $40 million. While he didn't land the deal, he walked away with much more – the power of possibility.

Unstoppable, his next move changed the trajectory of his career. Coming across a home with a defaulted mortgage, he met the owners—a family in serious financial trouble and facing foreclosure. Acquiring the homeowners' note from their bank, Terry modified their loan so they could afford to keep their home.

He made a double-digit interest return on his investment and kept a family in their home. With that one decision, he become a self-made millionaire. From there, his portfolio flourished with one legendary deal after the next, including **one home that he acquired for free and turned into an asset worth $1M**, an inheritance for his daughters, and an audacious appetite for success all from learning how to "Be The Bank."

MULTIPLYING MILLIONAIRES AS A MENTOR

Completely disrupting the status quo, Terry became known in real estate circles as an investment icon. One of his most successful mentees invested **$700 in Terry's training and 72 hours later closed a commercial note deal working directly with a bank that made him a $1.2 million dollar profit in one hour.** For the last two decades, Terry has privately taught his clients the wealth building power of investing in bank notes. Under Terry's tutelage, they master the powerful wealth building strategies that banks use to control capital and real estate. As a result, his clients make more money per deal than any other real estate investors in the country. But bigger than that, they're doing it without using their own credit, capital, a real estate license, or borrowing money from banks. Instead, they become the bank.

While Terry's expertise has earned his clients multiple millions of dollars, the far-reaching effects of his work will be renowned for years to come. With every client's success story, he is deconstructing an oppressive economic system that is meant to minimize and marginalize the middle class and the poor. As the real estate and banking industries perpetuate the myth that people who don't have credit, capital, experience, or credentials can't buy a home for their families or become investors, Terry is debunking that lie—one bank foreclosure millionaire at a time.

A Note From Terry...

How will I help you make money, build wealth, GET RICH, and Be a Real Estate Millionaire?

I had to sit down and really think hard about what it is that I bring to the table being that I am a leading expert in my niche of buying 2nd loans from banks, helping homeowners facing foreclosure "Keep Their Homes", and I've been investing in real estate for 40 years.

I've invested all across the United States in six different markets including California, Arizona, Nevada, Illinois, New York, and Florida.

I will help you to achieve the American Dream. Here's how:

I provide financial empowerment, financial literacy, and education training to help you learn about cash flow, real estate, finance, building wealth, estate planning, and debt-free living through books, videos, challenges, and live streaming.

Financial literacy is the ability to understand the numbers and basic principles of real estate investing in finance. Financial education is the key to financial success, especially in today's world. It's extremely important that you learn about investing, real estate, homeownership, income-producing property, and how to build wealth.

Real estate is the greatest wealth builder of all time!

More millionaires have been created from real estate than any other industry. I have real estate software games and mobile apps that I've developed for iOs and Android smartphones that educate adults and children about real estate, investing, and financial concepts in business.

I've developed and created products to teach people how to increase, multiply, and have their own money work hard for them instead of working hard for the money.

The reality is nobody is going to get ahead getting paid by the hour, that's living paycheck to paycheck. You have to have equity in something, real estate, income-producing property, and/or a business to have any chance at having wealth.

It's just like the equity in our homes. We have equity in our homes and when they appreciate that is where the majority of wealth is across the country. For people working by the hour and who don't own a home, they need to figure out how to get ownership and equity. This is the only way to close the income inequality wealth gap in this country!

This is what I do. I will teach you about equity, intellectual property, ownership of your own business, ownership of your own homes, and income-producing real estate so you can make an impact financially on your and your family's life and so that you can live the life you truly deserve, that's free of financial limitations so that you can have abundance and prosperity.

In order for you to build and have wealth, you have to know how wealth is built and the predominant way wealth is made in this country is by owning real estate.

Unless you grew up around wealth, business, investing, property ownership, and real estate, you probably have never been taught how to achieve the American dream. This is what I do and this is what I teach.

This is what I bring to the table as your real estate mentor, coach, and trainer and I support you 100%.
If you have any further questions, let's talk at (916) 470-3869.
Wishing you Success, Wealth, Health, Happiness & Prosperity.

Terry Bontemps

BANK FORECLOSURE MILLIONAIRE™: THE BRAND

The world's premier bank foreclosure investor training and bank note buying education platform, Bank Foreclosure Millionaire™ is facilitating the greatest transfer of economic power the world will ever witness.

Led by founder, real estate investor, and self-made millionaire Terry Bontemps, the company teaches its groundbreaking methodology to his clients nationwide. Through immersive coaching and tech tools, Terry's students become fluent in the language of banking and the infinite power of owning defaulted bank notes. Known for catapulting their net worth into the millions, BFM enrollees bank in one strategic swoop what an average investor makes in a lifetime. **From $400,000 to $1.2 million in net profits—in a single transaction—Terry's students are changing the trajectory of their finances and their families' futures forever.**

Wealth eludes most people because they are missing the savvy, the strategy, the mentorship, the consistency, and the know-how! Terry has dedicated the last 20 years of his life creating wealth breakthroughs for everyday people—people with families, dreams, aspirations, bills, and a true desire to live the American Dream.

Mentoring & Coaching

With unrivaled results, our immersive programs turn students into real-estate moguls, generational wealth builders, and money masters. Diving deep into the intricacies of commercial and residential real estate investing, bank notes, and foreclosures that aren't taught anywhere else, our enrollees acquire proven wealth building strategies, achieve financial freedom, and learn estate planning strategies that protect their assets and pass on wealth to future generations.

BANK FORECLOSURE MILLIONAIRE™ REAL ESTATE INVESTMENT EDUCATION SOFTWARE

Making millions has never been more fun with the development of Terry's mobile app, Bank Foreclosure Millionaire™.

Putting the foundations of our curriculum in the palm of your hand, our first-of-its-kind app brings players into a simulated world of high-stakes real estate investing, bank notes, and wealth building. As you master the stay-on-your-toes strategies and math that makes millions, it will be clear why, in this highly interactive game, players learn how to invest in real estate, make money, build wealth, get rich, and become millionaires.

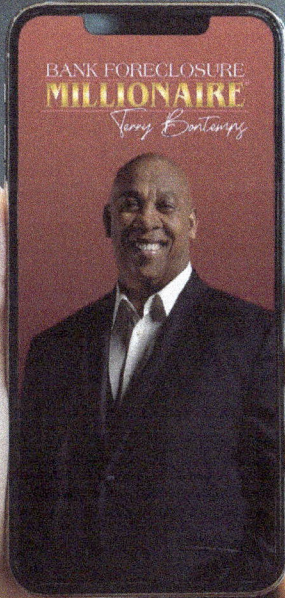

GET IN TOUCH

Terry Bontemps is frequently requested for interviews and speaking opportunities. His primary topics include wealth building through real estate, bank note buying, and foreclosures. He is currently open to new collaborations, interviews, and media features.

To request an interview with Terry, please contact the Bank Foreclosure Millionaires team at (916) 470-3869.

"WAY TOO MANY PEOPLE BELIEVE THAT
YOU NEED TO HAVE GOOD OR GREAT CREDIT
TO START INVESTING IN REAL ESTATE,
AND IT'S SIMPLY NOT TRUE.
You have been locked out of the wealth-building
experience due to what you didn't know!"

Have you ever thought to yourself you need a **boat load of cash to invest in real estate?** GUESS WHAT, it's simply **not true**!

Your family's legacy, well-being, and happiness are all impacted because of the **biggest myths** you've ever been told about real estate.

MYTH #1

The biggest myth around investing in real estate is that you need to use your own money.

The truth is that most real estate billionaires are using someone else's money, and it's TIME for you to learn how to do the same thing.

MYTH #2

You need good/great credit to invest in real estate.

Fact: Your credit is not even considered when using the **Bank Foreclosure Millionaire™ method.**

MYTH #3

You need to be a real estate expert to invest in real estate.

Haven't you ever wondered, "**What does it actually take to be wealthy and become a millionaire?"**

Maybe, you tried starting a business and that didn't cut it. You worked 40+ hours a week and that didn't cut it either.

You tried saving a little here and investing a little there, and it still didn't cut it.

This is the reason why I created **Bank Foreclosure Millionaire™**. This specifically designed system was created to fit your unique lifestyle. Whether you're a **do-it-yourself go-getter,** the type of person who learns better in a **communal environment,** or the type of person who needs one-on-one mentoring, I have the program for you.

Bank Foreclosure Millionaire™ is the world's most intensive, comprehensive, educational training course ever offered in the real estate industry. It's going to radically uplevel your financial destiny. Best of all, you'll be learning directly from me, the No. 1 bank foreclosure mentor in the world. It's perfect for those of you who are totally new to the business, or those seasoned pros looking for greater wealth opportunities.

Ok, let's deal with the elephant in the room. You're scared, skeptical, and suspicious, which is why **it's time** for you to conquer your fears with **the most extensive and in-depth, no fluff, and easy-to- understand** real estate wealth-building training that you have ever been a part of.

You've always wanted to try your hand at real estate. You've always wanted to provide for your family and, honestly, you're just tired of living on the edge financially.

It's time for change.

It's time for action, not self-doubt.

It's time for follow-through, as opposed to another missed opportunity. It's time for *Wealth For The Rest Of Us!*

For most people, wealth has eluded them because they were missing

- **The Savvy**
- **The Strategy**
- **The Mentorship**
- **The Consistency** and
- **The Know-How**

That all changes today! Here's how you can get started on *your own wealth-building journey:*

1. Create a space in your home or office dedicated to your learning. You'll need it in the coming weeks.

2. Download my **Bank Foreclosure Millionaire™** app and take your Wealth Teacher and Millionaire Mentor Terry Bontemps with you wherever you go.

3. Be committed. Everyday students like you are mastering the **Bank Foreclosure Millionaire™** blueprint.

Wishing you success, health, wealth, happiness, and prosperity!

Terry Bontemps

WISHING YOU SUCCESS,
HEALTH, WEALTH, HAPPINESS
AND PROSPERITY!

—Terry Bontemps

IT'S TIME FOR YOU TO *become a* BANK FORECLOSURE MILLIONAIRE

without using your own money.

The wealth building experience you've been waiting for 3 easy choices to fit your lifestyle

#ReadyForWealth

SIGN UP TODAY

BANK
FORECLOSURE ENTREPRENEUR

Start Your Wealth Journey Today

EXPERIENCE THE BANK
FORECLOSURE MILLIONAIRE WAY
CALL TERRY

Connect with Terry
(916) 470-3869

245

THERE ARE WAY TOO MANY PEOPLE

WHO BELIEVE

that you need to have good or great credit to start INVESTING in real estate and it's simply NOT TRUE.

You have been locked out of the

WEALTH BUILDING EXPERIENCE
DUE TO WHAT YOU DIDN'T KNOW

THE BIGGEST
MYTH

around investing in real estate is that you need to use your own money

THE TRUTH IS

Fact: that most real estate billionaires are using someone else's money and its TIME for you to learn how to do the same thing

MYTH NUMBER 2

I need good/great
credit to invest
in real estate

Fact: Your credit is not even
considered when using
the "BANK FORECLOSURE
MILLIONAIRE METHOD"

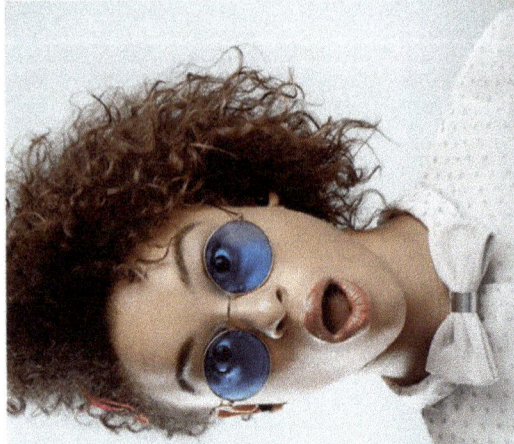

MYTH NUMBER 3

I need to be a
real estate expert
to invest in real estate

Fact: We can have you ready to
purchase your 1st Bank
Foreclosure Note in under
72 Hours using

THE BANK FORECLOSURE

MILLIONAIRE METHOD

It's time for

#WealthForTheRestofUs

Now is the time to **GENERATE REAL WEALTH BY INVESTING IN BANK FORECLOSURES**

For most,
wealth has eluded us because we were missing

THE SAVVY,

THE STRATEGY,

THE MENTORSHIP,

THE CONSISTENCY,

AND THE KNOW-HOW.

THAT ALL CHANGES TODAY

BANK FORECLOSURE MILLIONAIRE SYSTEM

IS GOING TO RADICALLY UPLEVEL YOUR *Financial Destiny.*

BEST OF ALL YOU WILL BE LEARNING
from the world's leading Bank Foreclosure

Mentor Terry Bontemps.

It's perfect for those who are totally new or those seasoned pros looking for **GREATER WEALTH OPPORTUNITIES.**

LEARN HOW TO:

- PURCHASE FORECLOSURE NOTES AT A DISCOUNT FROM BANKS
- BE THE BANK WITHOUT USING YOUR OWN MONEY
- EARN DOUBLE DIGIT - TRIPLE DIGIT RETURNS ON YOUR INVESTMENT

Start Your Wealth Journey Today

EXPERIENCE THE BANK
FORECLOSURE MILLIONAIRE WAY
CALL TERRY

✆ **Connect with Terry**
(916) 470-3869

BANK FORECLOSURE MILLIONAIRE SYSTEM

IS BROKEN DOWN INTO 3 SIMPLE OPTIONS

OPTION 1

The Bank Foreclosure

Millionaire Home Study Course

This allows you to learn at your own speed with the **MINIMUM INVESTMENT** while learning from the World's Number 1 Bank Foreclosure Expert

TERRY BONTEMPS

$20

Bank Foreclosure Millionaire App Only Download from App Store or Amazon No Training Materials Included

OPTION 2

The Bank Foreclosure

Millionaire Mastermind

This Mastermind is live and we reveal all of the secrets, all of **OUR BEST TACTICS, TIPS, AND TRICKS**

All of our best strategies designed to help get you going and get you on the path to wealth. You're going to love being a part of the **BANK FORECLOSURE COMMUNITY**

$4,997

Bank Foreclosure Millionaire App Must Be Purchased Separately. Training Materials Included

OPTION 3

The Bank Foreclosure

Millionaire One-On-One Mentoring Program

I get it, you're ready for the next level. You have no time to waste and you're committed to doing whatever it takes to becoming a **BANK FORECLOSURE MILLIONAIRE**

This is a unique opportunity for 10 people to be personally mentored by Terry Bontemps

BANK FORECLOSURE GURU & WEALTH EXPERT

$6,997

Bank Foreclosure Millionaire App Must Be Purchased Separately. Training Materials Included

****

THE
BANK FORECLOSURE MILLIONAIRE
APP IS THE HOME STUDY COURSE
****

BANK FORECLOSURE MILLIONAIRE
MOBILE APP

It's highly recommended that you purchase Bank Foreclosure Millionaire from Amazon or the Apple Store for $20

The real estate investing education game that Terry's developed will fully compliment the HOME STUDY COURSE, MILLIONAIRE MASTERMIND, 1on1 MENTORING PROGRAM videos, spreadsheets, templates and training materials

THE MOBILE APP IS NOT INCLUDED WITH THE PURCHASE OF ANY COURSE

**Bank Foreclosure Millionaire mobile app must be purchased separately from Amazon or the Apple Store **

Start Your Wealth Journey Today

EXPERIENCE THE BANK
FORECLOSURE MILLIONAIRE WAY
CALL TERRY

☏ **Connect with Terry**
(916) 470-3869

253

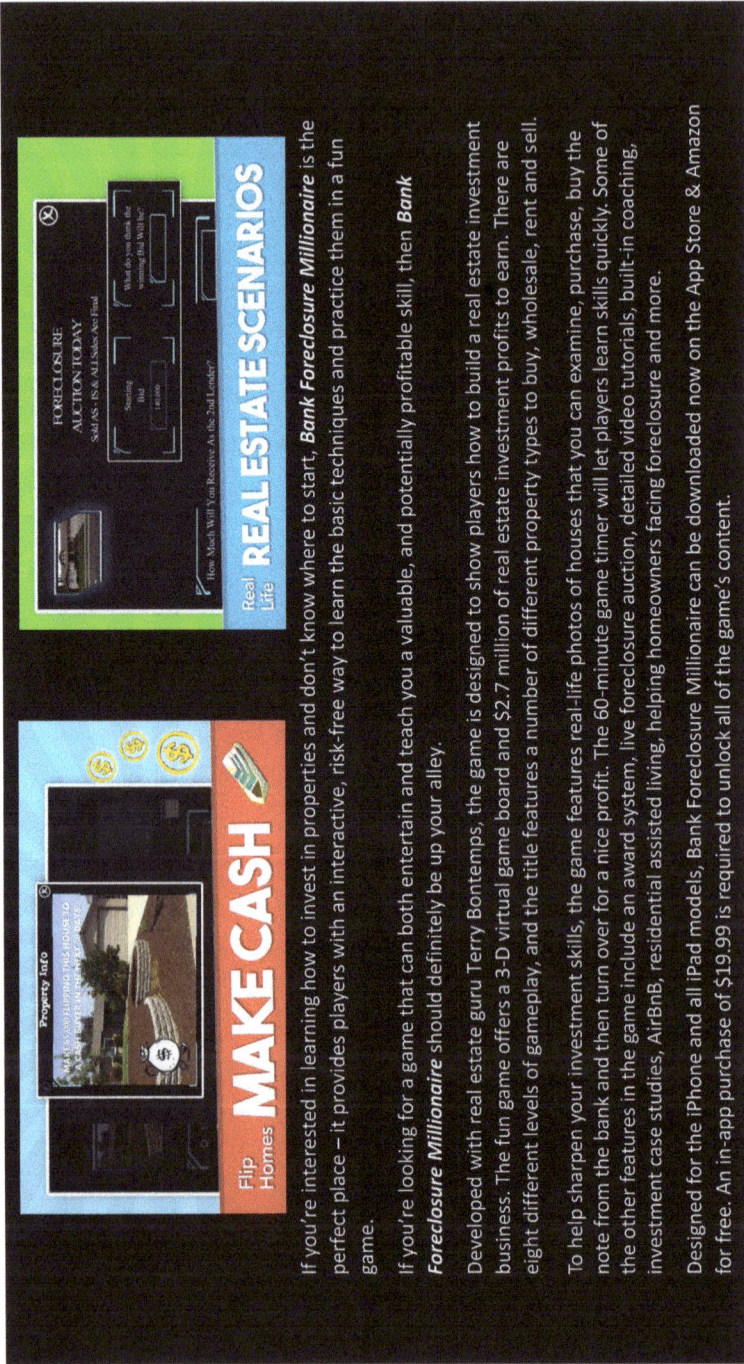

Flip Homes — **MAKE CASH**

Real Life — **REAL ESTATE SCENARIOS**

If you're interested in learning how to invest in properties and don't know where to start, *Bank Foreclosure Millionaire* is the perfect place – it provides players with an interactive, risk-free way to learn the basic techniques and practice them in a fun game.

If you're looking for a game that can both entertain and teach you a valuable, and potentially profitable skill, then *Bank Foreclosure Millionaire* should definitely be up your alley.

Developed with real estate guru Terry Bontemps, the game is designed to show players how to build a real estate investment business. The fun game offers a 3-D virtual game board and $2.7 million of real estate investment profits to earn. There are eight different levels of gameplay, and the title features a number of different property types to buy, wholesale, rent and sell.

To help sharpen your investment skills, the game features real-life photos of houses that you can examine, purchase, buy the note from the bank and then turn over for a nice profit. The 60-minute game timer will let players learn skills quickly. Some of the other features in the game include an award system, live foreclosure auction, detailed video tutorials, built-in coaching, investment case studies, AirBnB, residential assisted living, helping homeowners facing foreclosure and more.

Designed for the iPhone and all iPad models, Bank Foreclosure Millionaire can be downloaded now on the App Store & Amazon for free. An in-app purchase of $19.99 is required to unlock all of the game's content.

Investing in real estate seems like a pretty straight forward way to get rich. All you need to do is buy an ugly house, paint it so that it becomes a pretty house, and sell it for twice what you paid - right?

WRONG. Real estate is a great way to make a fortune and win your financial independence, but it's a complicated game – full of arcane terms and complex deal structures. You need a guide, a coach or a mentor.

Enter *Bank Foreclosure Millionaire*, a monopoly-esque digital boardgame created by successful property developer Terry Bontemps that aims to be educational and fun. In fact, it is possibly the best app out there on how to learn how to profit in real estate.

Making Bank...

Each turn gives you an hour to make as much money as you can by buying, renovating, managing, wholesaling, "being the bank" and selling properties to a variety of different purchaser types – from banks to hedge funds to private owners to landlords.

Through a straightforward quiz format, the game teaches you essential skills such as how to structure a deal, raise investment capital, and negotiate with buyers and sellers.

It also shows how to identify a likely property and conduct an all-important financial analysis that let's you know whether you should buy or avoid it.

Bank Foreclosure Millionaire Could Make You Rich...

There's a huge variety of different transaction types to get your head around, including multi-family houses, fixer uppers, probate properties, note buying, short sales, fire damaged buildings, luxury homes, and the all-important foreclosure auction.

This all may sound a little dry, but here's the clever part: despite giving you a comprehensive education in the complex world of real estate transactions, *Bank Foreclosure Millionaire* is never dull.

Thanks to it's jazzy 3D presentation and slick quiz format, it plays like any other addictive, fast paced touchscreen boardgame. It just teaches you how to become a millionaire along the way. Who can complain about that?

LEARN REAL ESTATE INVESTING

Flip This House
Real Estate Investing Game...

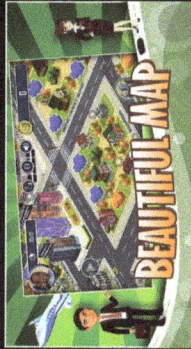

BEAUTIFUL MAP

Real Life Real Estate Scenarios...

EASY CALCULATION

MOVE OVER MONOPOLY! Learning how to invest in real estate and make big profits buying houses at a low price, fixing them up, and then selling them at a higher price while focusing on making solid financial decisions is as easy as playing a highly addictive, challenging and fun real estate investing education game.

With the innovative new educational app, *Bank Foreclosure Millionaire*, players will actually learn in a fast way how to make money, build wealth, get rich and be a real estate millionaire without risking real money during 60 minutes of highly profitable interactive game play.

People from all over the country watch television shows, read books, buy coaching programs and attend high cost seminars that highlight the ins and outs of real estate investment.

However, taking that newfound knowledge and putting it to the test in the real world can be daunting and result in failed investment opportunities. With the educational game *Bank Foreclosure Millionaire*, players are able to actually learn real life, realistic investment strategies and then practice those strategies buying, fixing, managing rentals, & flipping houses in a safe and fun way with no financial risk, prior to attempting it on their own in the real world.

The detailed gameplay includes a 3D virtual game board, $2.7 million dollars of real estate investment profits to earn, 8 levels of highly interactive game play, dozens of different property types to buy and sell, and real-life photos of real houses to examine, purchase, and turn over for profit.

Bank Foreclosure Millionaire is the only highly-interactive, profit-filled real estate investment training in the world driven by game based learning which gives you the best educational experience possible," says creator Terry Bontemps.

This amazing and addicting game features an on-going award system, fun animation, a live foreclosure auction, 342 interactive algorithms, detailed video tutorials, built-in personal coaching from a millionaire real estate mentor, real life investment case studies, a personal bank account to deposit your profit checks and a 60 minute game timer, which is all the time needed to learn the tricks of the trade!

Learn the secrets of real estate tycoons and download *Bank Foreclosure Millionaire* today from the App Store or Amazon!

Make Money **FLIPPING HOUSES**

Bank Foreclosure Millionaire is free to download from the App Store or Google Play.

The app was developed by famed investment guru Terry Bontemps (https://www.youtube.com/user/ib uyhouses1

The app will actually teach players how to build their real estate fortune and make their investing dreams come true.

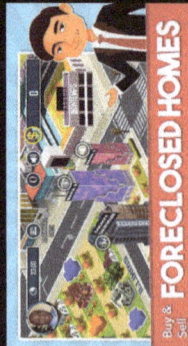

Buy & Sell **FORECLOSED HOMES**

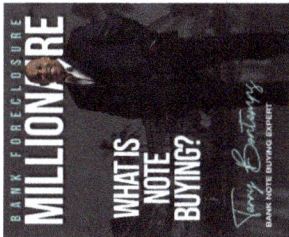

BANK FORECLOSURE MILLIONAIRE

WHAT IS NOTE BUYING?

includes the following 10 training modules (over 271 pages)

which are to be used in conjunction with Level 4 of

TERRY'S BANK FORECLOSURE MILLIONAIRE

MOBILE APP

MODULE #1	MODULE #2	MODULE #3	MODULE #4	MODULE #5
House Flipping Game Instruction Manual (40 pages)	Key Performance Indicators Manual (22 pages)	We Help You Keep Your Home Manual (26 pages)	Forms and Documents Manual (23 pages)	$40,000 Profit in ONE HOUR Manual Vol 1 (21 pages)

MODULE #6	MODULE #7	MODULE #8	MODULE #9	MODULE #10
$40,000 Profit in ONE HOUR Manual Vol 2 (21 pages)	$40,000 Profit in ONE HOUR Presentation Handout (24 pages)	What is Note Buying Manual (22 pages)	$40,000 Profit in ONE HOUR Power Point Presentation (12 pages)	11 Steps to Note Buying Success Manual (80 pages)

257

BANK FORECLOSURE MILLIONAIRE

HIGHLY INTERACTIVE WEALTH PLAYBOOK

is a digital download. It includes

38+ Value Packed Training Video Links (5+ hours), 11 Coaching Modules

14 deal analysis spreadsheets and 13 excel models

** Financial Spreadsheets and Excel Software Templates ARE INCLUDED WITH THIS TRAINING **

Terry has already built and developed the spreadsheets, templates and software that you'll need

****
INCLUDED WITH THE
MASTERMIND & MENTORING
TRAINING
****

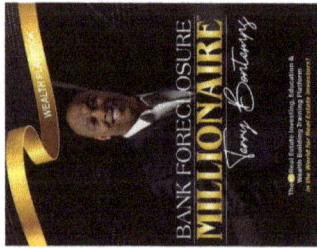

Start Your Wealth Journey Today

EXPERIENCE THE BANK
FORECLOSURE MILLIONAIRE WAY
CALL TERRY

Connect with Terry
(916) 470-3869

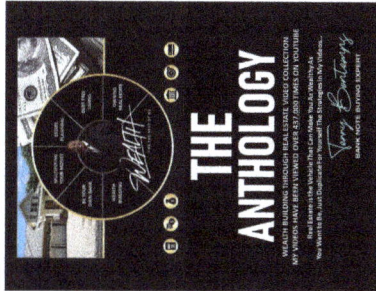

BUILD YOUR WEALTH
BUYING FORECLOSURES
FROM BANKS

5 DAY CHALLENGE

is a 7 hour video training course that
Terry Bontemps personally taught on
"How to Buy Foreclosure Properties Directly
from Banks for 30% to 50% Below Market Value
Without Using Your Own Money or Credit"

I'M READY TO BE THE BANK

Day #1
Homeowners and
Landlords Facing
Foreclosure

Day #2
Buy The Note -
Be The Bank &
GET RICH

Day #3
11 Steps to Build
Your Wealth
Buying
Foreclosures
From Banks

Day #4
How to Build
Wealth Buying
Notes Without
Cash or Credit

Day #5
7 Profitable Ways
to Build Wealth
Buying Notes
From Banks

****
INCLUDED WITH THE
MASTERMIND & MENTORING
TRAINING
****

Start Your Wealth Journey Today

EXPERIENCE THE BANK
FORECLOSURE MILLIONAIRE WAY
CALL TERRY

☏ **Connect with Terry**
(916) 470-3869

260

Wealth Path

$6,997

BANK FORECLOSURE MILLIONAIRE ONE-ON-ONE MENTORING

(LIMITED TO 10 PEOPLE)

This level includes 2 ONE-ON-ONE mentoring calls a week. The calls will be held Monday through Friday at the convenience of the client.

ONE-ON-ONE mentoring calls will be for 1 year. Terry will personally give instructions on how to progress through the BANK FORECLOSURE MILLIONAIRE COURSE. Terry will also be answering client's personal questions on the mentoring call. **BANK FORECLOSURE MILLIONAIRE** is a self- paced course. Client can go as fast as they want or as slow as needed.

WHEN MOST PEOPLE THINK ABOUT REAL ESTATE THEY

THINK ABOUT THE PHYSICAL STRUCTURE

AND NOT

THE NOTE!!

LEARNING HOW TO PURCHASE BANK FORECLOSURE NOTES is the SECRET to CRACKING the *Wealth Code.*

It's the never told story about how the banks got rich

I'M READY TO LEARN
Register Now Click Here

Start Your Wealth Journey Today

Connect with Terry
(916) 470-3869

EXPERIENCE THE BANK
FORECLOSURE MILLIONAIRE WAY
CALL TERRY

263

HOW DO I GET STARTED
with my wealth journey

Choose the option that aligns with you

Check your email, including your spam box

I'm going to personally text you. It's time to get the wealth conversation started

Create a space in your home or office dedicated to your learning. You'll need it in the coming weeks

Pay it forward. Share it with a friend or family member

Download the app and take your wealth mentor wherever you go

Be committed. Everyday students like you are mastering the Bank Foreclosure Millionaire Blueprint

Start Your Wealth Journey Today

EXPERIENCE THE BANK
FORECLOSURE MILLIONAIRE WAY
CALL TERRY

📞 Connect with Terry
(916) 470-3869

DON'T WORRY ABOUT THE MONEY, DON'T WORRY ABOUT THE CREDIT.

We're going to teach you everything you need to know about how to get started investing, making money and building wealth owning real estate.

We are an advocate for

the wealth champion in you

Start Your Wealth Journey Today

EXPERIENCE THE BANK
FORECLOSURE MILLIONAIRE WAY
CALL TERRY

📞 **Connect with Terry**
(916) 470-3869

265

My Name is

Terry Bontemps

and I didn't know what I didn't know when it came to generating wealth. Like many others before me I thought I needed to get loans from banks, have money, good credit and previous investing experience. When all I actually needed was the know-how.

So, I started learning everything I could about Bank Foreclosure Notes. I went from the student, to the teacher, to the expert, to the World's #1 Bank Foreclosure Note Buying Expert.

I was able to rescue my family from a life of hardship. I was able to finally start living the lifestyle I only dreamed about. I was able to create true freedom and happiness all because I was willing, ready and committed. So, I have a question for you. Are you ready? Are you willing? Are you committed to building generational wealth for you and your family?

If the answer is yes, then welcome to the first day of your new life as a Bank Foreclosure Champion. Together we can co-create the wealth destiny you've always imagined.

📞 Connect with Terry
(916) 470-3869

Start Your Wealth Journey Today

EXPERIENCE THE BANK
FORECLOSURE MILLIONAIRE WAY
CALL TERRY

266

"If You Don't Come from A Wealthy Family, Then A Wealthy Family Needs To Come From You"

-Michael Dalcoe

WEALTH

FOR THE REST OF US

www.ingramcontent.com/pod-product-compliance
Lightning Source LLC
Chambersburg PA
CBHW052110030426
42335CB00025B/2913